M&A AT CENTER STAGE

DEALMAKING IN A NEW ECONOMY

BEST PRACTICES OF THE BEST DEALMAKERS
3RD EDITION

M&A AT CENTER STAGE
DEALMAKING IN A NEW ECONOMY

Preface by Richard A. Martin, Jr., Senior Director, Merrill DataSite
Letter From The Editor by David A. Fergusson, President & Co-CEO, The M&A Advisor
Introduction by Marshall Sonenshine, Chairman, Sonenshine Partners

Library of Congress Control Number: 2015913626
ISBN: 978-0-9898161-2-0

Printed in China

For more information about special discounts for bulk purchases in the United States by corporations, institutions, and other organizations please contact The M&A Advisor at 212-951-1550.

PRAISE FOR BEST PRACTICES OF THE BEST DEALMAKERS - 3RD EDITION

"Even the most experienced M&A professionals need to stay current with constantly evolving trends, innovative structures, and fresh developments in transaction markets. Best Practices of the Best Dealmakers is an invaluable resource, providing important, on-point information in a brief, accessible format."

– Michael S. Goldman, Managing Director,
TM Capital Corp.

"This third edition in the Best Practices of the Best Dealmakers provides a systematic approach to addressing critical issues in any M&A investment situation—such as how much to pay for the business and how to get the deal done. Many of the ground rules and subtlety of the M&A trade are often passed on orally from banker-to-banker on a case-by-case basis. This book series is helping to codify the art and science of investment banking. As with the previous two volumes, this edition is helping to convert the industry's oral tradition into a practical and user-friendly framework to master skills that are fundamental for any role in transaction-related finance."

– Brent D. Earles, Senior Vice President,
Allegiance Capital Corporation, Author
H&R Block's Just Plain Smart book series

"The 'Best Practices' book is a unique collection of ideas and experiences of seasoned dealmakers with a track record of transaction excellence. A great read for any professional."

– Patrick O'Keefe, Founder and CEO, O'Keefe

"Essential reading for anyone doing M&A in today's complex deal-making environment. The book provides in depth, valuable insight into best practice execution and strategies to maximize the outcome of any transaction."

– Justine Mannering, Managing Director, BDA

"This edition of Best Practices reads like a living room conversation with leading professionals and investors who are involved in some of the biggest and most complicated deals. A valuable resource for anyone involved in M&A transactions."

– Geoffrey T. Raicht, Partner, Proskauer

"The world of Cross-Border M&A combines the skill sets one acquires over a lifetime. Bridging cultural and business practices and the meshing of legal and financial systems in different stages of maturation. Best Practices of the Best Dealmakers is an invaluable and highly practical tool in navigating that process and creating a bridge to an integrated global economy."

– Selig D. Sacks, Co-Chair, International Practice Group, Foley & Lardner LLP

"I highly recommend this series to anyone considering a career in finance or investment – or anyone who thinks they know how to get a deal done."

– David Hellier, Partner, Bertram Capital

CONTENTS

PREFACE

Best Practices of the Best Dealmakers, 3rd Edition, is the third major publishing effort between Merrill DataSite and The M&A Advisor. The Best Practices book series explores the state-of-the art M&A methodology in today's dealmaking. Its approach combines a direct approach to the fundamentals of M&A and presents it through the wisdom of the dealmakers themselves. Our contributors have vast experience in the field. We are indebted to their collaboration in this effort to share best practices with the entire M&A community.

For Merrill DataSite, the Best Practices series reflects our long partnership with the financial industry. In addition to supporting the industry's best practices, Merrill DataSite has served as a partner and as a source of education to M&A dealmakers, producing and sharing academic-quality white papers and how-to guides with our customers to keep them abreast of industry trends while offering practical instruction on ways to cope with marketplace challenges. Likewise, our partner, The M&A Advisor, recognizes and promotes the achievements of the industry's premier deal teams, firms and dealmakers.

The collaboration between Merrill DataSite and The M&A Advisor is constructed on a common focus and passion: to present the principles of successful dealmaking and to share those principles broadly in a comprehensive guide. Our publication seeks to relate the established methodologies employed universally by successful dealmakers with the overarching goal to provide M&A professionals with an essential and timeless dealmaking reference tool.

Best Practices of the Best Dealmakers, 3rd Edition fully expresses that purpose. After years of slow recovery from the greatest financial crisis since the Great Depression, M&A activity has rebounded to a robust level. This latest installment in our Best Practices book series shows how dealmakers are adapting their traditional deal execution methodologies to fit the new, rapid pace of M&A activity.

We are indebted to the many colleagues and peers who provided the guidance, input and hard work necessary to produce this book. I would like to thank

Catherine Malone and the Merrill DataSite team for their on-going dedication and for applying their high level of exactitude to this endeavor.

I would also like to thank Roger Aguinaldo and David Fergusson of The M&A Advisor for again sharing their industry knowledge, resources and contacts from around the world. Finally, I would like to thank all the M&A professionals who contributed their time and their valuable insights to the third installment of our Best Practices series.

Richard A. Martin, Jr
Senior Director
Merrill DataSite

LETTER FROM THE EDITOR

I t seems longer really, but just four years ago the economy was still moribund in the aftermath of the global financial crisis. M&A activity was only just beginning to pick up from the lows of the Great Recession. Yet, even in such a gloomy economic climate, we were recognizing continued and consistent high performance from the best-in-class dealmakers.

The response to our first "Best Practices of The Best Dealmakers" report in 2012 was overwhelmingly positive and we were encouraged to continue to research, write and publish this chronicle of insight and perspective on the best practices for M&A, restructuring and financing in the post-crisis era.

The collaboration between Merrill DataSite and The M&A Advisor to engage the artful practitioners of our trade in conversations about what they are doing and why, has resulted in a regular series of reports throughout the year, and the culmination of our analysis into a book at year's end.

In 2014, mergers and acquisitions reached levels unseen in more than 10 years, and we have been witness to the value of chronicling the best-in-class performance of our industry's professionals. In this, the 3rd edition of Best Practices of the Best Dealmakers, we catalogue and celebrate the wisdom of the industry leaders whose perseverance and ingenuity has kept them on top.

I am very appreciative of the 43 professionals – women and men who are leading our industry, who have generously contributed their time and their candid views about the opportunities and challenges they have encountered, the strategies and tactics they have engaged, and their results.

To Richard Martin, Senior Director of Merrill DataSite, whose vision for this initiative and steadfast commitment to enabling the M&A industry to perform at the highest level, I am so grateful.

This book has also benefitted greatly from the historical and intellectual contributions of Marshall Sonenshine, Chairman of Sonenshine Partners and Professor of Finance at Columbia University. Thank you for sharing your expertise and perspective.

Tom Allen and Andy Yemma, our writers for the 3rd edition, have been inquisitive and sensitive, thoughtful and thorough in their engagement with the book's contributors. Their professionalism, a compliment echoed by all who they communicated with, became a hallmark for this project. For that, I am incredibly appreciative.

I also want to recognize the invaluable contributions to this initiative by my business partner and our company's founder, Roger Aguinaldo. It has been a pleasure to engage with him and draw on his dealmaking and deal watching experience. He has amassed a wealth of knowledge that this series has benefitted greatly from.

I believe I am very fortunate to have the opportunity to curate this program. Over this past year, I have proudly reported conversations with the country's leading dealmakers about proven best practices in our annual think tank summits, and on the stages of other forums and academic institutions. I continue to learn from and be inspired by the financial services professionals whose contribution to the economic marketplace extends well beyond our industry.

Last, I am thankful to have been able to share the results of these thoughtful conversations with you, our readers, leaders, and colleagues. I look forward to continue to engage with you in this ongoing dialogue.

David A. Fergusson
Editor
Best Practices of the Best Dealmakers, 3rd Edition

INTRODUCTION

The Genesis of Deal Making - Strategy

In M&A, the playbook for virtually all participants, whether corporate or financial, is now strategic. Things were not always this way. Bankers who came of age during the halcyon days of leveraged finance generally ran two playbooks in tandem: Strategic and Financial.

The Strategic playbook asked the question about which corporate buyers could acquire a company and what changes would they make to the company's management, strategy or operation, to add synergy value that would justify the strategic price that the target company would cost. The Financial playbook asked how we could change the capital structure of the firm, principally through leverage, to cause the firm to focus more intensively on cash flow for purposes of reducing leverage and enhancing equity value over time. Private equity-led buyouts trace their origins to this simple playbook.[1]

The second playbook, while not extinct, is less useful today than in the past. Today, financial buyers must think strategically because most acquisition prices are too high to rely solely on financial engineering to generate excess returns above public market equivalents. In the early years of this transition, private equity firms began adding operating partners to their ranks, drawn from industry, to help improve portfolio companies operationally and strategically, thus enhancing revenues and profits. As they added operating partners, PE funds developed sector expertise and core competency expertise towards strategic value enhancement. Highly interventionist funds have tended to generate higher returns than those that relied on the principally financial engineering.

On both sides of the old Strategic/Financial divide, everyone must now be a strategist. Further, the M&A market itself is now considerably more driven by corporate than PE buyouts. Financial deal making constituted some 30% of global mergers pre-2008 Financial Crisis, but in the years since then aggregate deal volume appears to have recovered toward the $4 trillion level as of this writing in 2015, but the percentage of M&A attributable to private

---

1. See M. Jensen, "Eclipse of the Public Corporation," Harvard Business School (1989).

equity remains significantly down. Further, financial buyouts include some companies that get re-sold to other PE firms, suggesting they are simply best owned this way, and others that are transacted by financial firms with relevant portfolio companies, i.e. with strategic motivations. Hence, the brave new world of M&A is actually a return to an older world of corporate mergers: The deal is about strategy.

All this raises the question, what is strategy and how do deals enhance strategy? There are many definitions to each of these, and as a 28-year veteran of the industry and a longstanding professor at Columbia Business School I am happy to add my own sense of these broad concepts. For these purposes, corporate strategy is the art of configuration; that is, how one configures a company to optimize its performance within that sector. By configure we mean not merely capitalization, nor even management, but what business assets are organized around what business relationships and game plans so as to win both the battle for market share and the war for shareholder value. To navigate these heady issues, one must deal with not just finance but also commerce – questions around management, product development, sales and marketing, competition, operations, technology, strategy. One can no longer be a dealmaker in a financial silo; one can only be a dealmaker in a far more complex and multi-dimensional business matrix.

I expect the reader of the M&A Advisor's *Best Practices of the Best Dealmakers, 3rd Edition* will detect a high degree of similar thinking and stories about strategy and synergy underlying corporate deal making. That is a reflection of where we are now in the multidisciplinary professions of corporate mergers. That is because in the decade following the greatest financial crisis in eight decades, now we are all strategists.

The Art of Dealmaking

The typical arc of the deal is social at the front end, adversarial during key inflection points, and obsessive in the final stages. In this respect, the front end of the deal is arguably the most fun part, the creative part, and the visionary part. The parties know that if they proceed they will find areas for conflict over price, terms, control of the company, et cetera. And they know that as those elements come to rest, their counsel and teams will engage in rituals of obsession over legal, financial, accounting and other matters. But in the earliest acts of the drama, the deal is social.

Indeed, the language of the early stages of dealmaking reflects the essential social character of the work. There is an "approach." The topic is "socialized." Parties establish a "relationship", which is not a relationship in the personal sense, but a transitory business relationship that might be able to facilitate the mix of collaborative and adversarial interactions that dealmaking requires. A "dialogue" ensues. In other words, the parties are doing the deal.

Deal people know these interactions have ritualistic and tactical designs as well as uncertain elements that can upend those plans. They are on high alert even when they are pretending to be casual in phone calls and meetings and dinners in various cities. This is part of the work of dealmaking, part of the charm of it.

The essays and interviews that follow vet the early stages of dealmaking, from strategizing to socializing to exploring to vetting to documenting letters of intent or memoranda of understanding.

The letter of intent (LOI) or memorandum of understanding (MOU) is another area of some debate. Many deals are best done without any LOI or MOU for the simple reason that the document is often not binding anyway. In those situations, once a price and a few other basic terms are in place, it may be efficient not to interpose another area of conflict when one can go straight to the only document that really matters, the definitive agreement. This may be sensible where the parties know exactly what they are doing, while in other situations the interposed LOI may be necessary to avoid chaos. Here again, one makes judgments based on the specific facts of a case, not some imaginary playbook for all games.

Perhaps most important, the deal process must house both conflict and collaboration, since all deals have both ingredients. Dealmakers understand this and they behave accordingly. In some moments one invites the other side to a five-star dinner; days later, one may abruptly end a call or meeting with an epithet thrown in for effect. As noted, these dynamics are not exactly what are generally meant (at least for this author) by the word "relationship," but deal relationships bring people together for a very particular purpose – doing a deal.

For most companies, the deal is an interruption to the ordinary course of business; only for dealmakers is deal-making the ordinary course. Thus, dealmakers are an unusual lot. For us, the ebb and the flow of deal interactions are colorful and opportunistic, much as is the case for trial lawyers and politicians. Opportunities often occur in the maelstrom, the vortex of multiple parties with their multiple agendas.

Getting to the Close

Some thirty years ago, as a second-year law student, I took a course called "Negotiation", taught by the late Roger Fisher. His iconic negotiation manual, appropriately entitled *Getting to Yes*[2], was on the reading list. Fisher, a professor at Harvard Law School, was co-author of the book with William Ury, a professor at Harvard Business School. Of all my law school books, *Getting to Yes* is both the shortest and the one with the longest shelf life. The book would soon take its place in my library with two other brilliant short books that tell essential truths concisely.[3]

The question is what practices make for success in M&A. What, then, can one say about "Getting to Yes" specifically in the context of doing M&A deals? Reflecting on Fisher's and Ury's wisdom and my own accumulated experience in M&A, I would offer the following eight succinct observations as introduction to the current volume of *Best Practices of the Best Dealmakers*.

First, if at all possible, avoid being eagerly obsessed with one counterparty. Those with options generally negotiate better than those without options. Too many sellers of companies think they can "find the right buyer" and then focus exclusively on that party.

Second, understand the full myriad of issues that create an economic deal. The most salient but not sole issue is price. Other issues include form of consideration, structure, management incentives, terms and conditions in a stock or asset Purchase Agreement, capital structure, speed, certainty, and other topics.

Third, understand how the other side bargains. We spent considerable time in my class at Harvard assessing different styles of negotiation, from "positional" negotiators (meaning those who take starting positions they intend to negotiate significantly) to "principled" negotiators, who state principles (broad or tailored) that animate their negotiation.

---

2. See R. Fisher and W. Ury, Getting to Yes (Penguin Group, 1981).

3. The other two great short works in my library are Peter Drucker's The Effective Executive and William Strunck and E.B. White's grammar and usage manual, The Elements of Style. I suspect few readers today read all, or perhaps even any of these, but I can honestly say that any professional would save himself or herself countless hours of frustration by reading all three. For those of us who lead, write and negotiate for a living, these form a working person's bible.

Fourth, measure not just the other side's words but also its behavior – and remember that often behavior matters more than words. I am constantly amazed at how many experienced lawyers, bankers, investors and executives will report on what a counterparty said, as though that were the greatest source of insight into his intent. We learn in life to evaluate conduct more than words.

Fifth, create contexts that can help win desired results. Some dealmakers just talk. Others orchestrate – and good orchestration can create good results for the orchestrator. We all do this to some extent, choosing where to seat oneself or others, or in what order to approach certain parties in a multilateral process or even within a particular company, all for tactical reasons. The late US Ambassador Richard Holbrooke was a master of theater. In negotiating the resolution to the Balkan War he had the Bosnian and Serbian leaders agree to meet him for cease-fire talks at a US Air Force base in Dayton Ohio. What he did not tell them is that dinner would be served on a white tablecloth in a hangar – with American B-52 bombers overhanging the table.

Sixth, understand that everything – even an auction – is a negotiation. Relatively few auctions for companies are true sealed bid auctions like silent auctions at a charity gala. Most are really a series of bilateral negotiations with the seller, and most finalists become negotiation counterparties in the course of an auction process.

Seventh, instead of following a canned protocol, do this very particular deal well. Instead of following a playbook, use all your God-given (or market-given) tools. Too many bankers think the process of doing a deal is rote.

Eighth, Remember Berra. As long as we are on the subject of psychology, one must remember the important words of baseball legend Yogi Berra: "90 percent of this game is half mental."

After the Closing

It is a curiosity of the deal business that dealmakers and companies mark the completion of a transaction with a "closing" dinner at which bankers present a memento of the deal in the form of a Lucite "tombstone." What happens after the last drink has been consumed and the last farewells expressed at an M&A closing dinner? What realities commence, at least for the principals, on the fateful Morning After? On the Morning After, the principals must manage the immediate requirements of the deal itself, the medium needs and opportunities of the acquired business, and the longer-term strategic demands for continuity and change in the life of the newly owned or combined corporation.

Beyond the medium term process of adding value and explaining it, is the longer term reality that businesses and markets, as all human enterprises, are always in flux. Whatever the vision at the time of the close, the vision will change because business and life change. The most successful deals are the ones that can manage continuity and change post close. This is a particular problem for corporate mergers, which are generally long term, as opposed to financial acquisitions, which are generally medium term bets, but it is one that all M&A participants face to some degree. We dealmakers love to close, but if we are self-aware, we know we really are agents not of closings, but of new beginnings, as my colleagues in the chapter that follows will elucidate. Here's to New Beginnings, which start after the Close.

Some Words on Anti-Trust and Activism

This new edition of Best Practices by The Best Dealmakers includes two special reports – one on the return of anti-trust activity and the other on the resurgence in investor activism in M&A.

It is not enough to say that major antitrust authorities in the US, Europe and elsewhere are today an increasingly active and potent force in global M&A. It is more important, at least in this forum, to say why that is and what this means for dealmakers on the front lines of business as well as what it means for the antitrust attorneys who try antitrust cases in the US and, now, worldwide. My perspective is that of a dealmaker who is trained as a lawyer.

In the US, there were halcyon days for antitrust, from the early 20th century trust-busting under the Sherman and Clayton Acts to much later cases that would define major American industries from movies to alcohol to computers. By contrast, for meaningful periods during the great bull market from 1988 to 2008, anti-trust enforcement was often quiescent, at times shrinking the standing army of anti-trust lawyers or at least sending some home early with nary a case to work on. In the years preceding the global financial crisis, the US Department of Justice allowed a half-decade to elapse without litigating a single merger case.

From a dealmaker's perspective, the era of quiescent antitrust enforcement is over. Anyone who doubted that assessment was rudely awakened in 2011 when the US government blocked AT&T from acquiring T-Mobile. So why have the antitrust authorities awakened? Part of the answer lies in the obvious fact of large-scale consolidations. Strategic M&A has continued strong, even if at reduced volumes post-financial crisis, and this year may drive a $3.5 trillion annualized global merger market if first half trends continue. Part of the explanation arguably resides with the long shadow cast by the financial crisis itself, which if nothing else stands for the proposition – however ironic in the age of continued banking consolidation – that where there is corporate scale there is public risk. Part of the answer might be found in tendency in the US for anti-trust policy to be more activist under Democratic than Republican administrations. There is also the stock market run-up, which facilitates stock mergers, testing concentration limits. And there is the market preference for pure plays, which facilitates spin-offs leaving companies to diversify less and concentrate (horizontally and vertically) more.

As with antitrust issues, some may sense déjà vu with today's rise in investor activism. Some years ago the idea of activism seemed non mainstream, akin to ambulance chasing. In the era of greenmail, activism was analogized to corporate extortion. That has changed, such that today shareholder activism broadly is part of the corporate finance landscape alongside companies, boards, bankers and investors. Like hostile takeover activity, which similarly was once thought of as impolitic or down market corporate behavior, activism has gone from often dodgy to generally mainstream.

The activist community includes many flavors just as all professional communities within financial markets do, whether banking, law, board, management or investor. One simply cannot say activists are "good" or "bad," constructive or destructive forces. They are all of the above and other things as well.

The rise in activism was facilitated in the 1990s by the SEC, which promulgated new shareholder proxy rules that made it easier and cheaper for stockholders to wage proxy fights. In the 2000s, particularly after the financial crisis of 2008, the continued growth in activism was driven by the market itself – the demand by public investors for value that corporations too often were not delivering. Hoarding cash became common corporate practice in the long recovery period after 2008, but activists often saw such hoarding as antithetical to shareholder interests and often successfully pressed for special dividends or at least board oversight to seek other forms of value enhancement.

What, then, can we say about activism from a dealmaker's perspective? First, one size does not fit all; activists are neither all good nor all bad. Second, activism creates a robust dynamic between corporate fiduciaries and corporate shareholders. Third, as activists stimulate possibilities for change, dealmakers may find increased latitude to drive change. Indeed, activists can be a dealmakers' tool. We should call the good activists "constructivists."

Corporate campaigns, like political ones, are not about activists versus directors, nor red versus blue states. They are about reason. Where companies have good reasons for resisting market sentiment, they should articulate those reasons. And where activists have a case, they can make it through the proxy machinery, the financial press, or wherever else they may speak. Democracy and capitalism are two sides of a coin: both bow to reason; both are a market for value.

Marshall Sonenshine
Chairman, Sonenshine Partners
Professor of Finance and Economics, Columbia University

ONE

Strategy and Synergy

Vital Elements of the Deal

Part I. Front-End M&A Strategy: Development and Execution

A. Strategy: The Foundation of the Deal

"Valuations are so high now that unschooled buyers are vulnerable to overpayment." – Andrew Lohmann, law firm Hirschler Fleisher

Sixty percent of M&A transactions fail to achieve their objective. The causes for the failure of these deals are several. Among them are the absence of an M&A strategy, having a strategy that is unaligned with corporate strategy, the sacrifice by buyer or seller of an M&A strategy's discipline and rigor while in hot pursuit of a transaction that may have ceased to be appropriate. Today, with acquisitions often commanding multiples in excess of 10X or 11X, compared to 8X just a couple of years ago, it behooves both buyers and sellers to enter the M&A marketplace with a clear plan.

This plan should take into account the changed realities of a supercharged marketplace that, in some respects, would be almost unrecognizable to the dealmakers from a decade earlier, when tandem deal playbooks for corporate and financial dealmakers were the norm, before evolving strategic considerations in an upside-down M&A marketplace induced dealmakers to exchange old playbooks and labels for membership in a single category: M&A strategist.

For corporate buyers and sellers, or for the 3,700 private equity firms whose combined impact remains, for now, on the ascendant in an overheating marketplace in which hungry and numerous corporate and private equity buyers scramble to gain the attention of a thinned herd of sellers, a comprehensive M&A strategy is necessary to help dealmakers identify achievable cost and revenue synergies.

"M&A does not represent a strategic goal in and of itself," cautions Simon Gisby, Managing Director, Deloitte Corporate Finance LLC, The M&A Advisor's 2014 Deal of the Year honoree in the healthcare/life sciences category. Instead, Gisby says, "It is a tactic upon which to achieve a broader strategic goal." The strategic objective can be financial, aimed, for example, at improving earnings per share. It can define a market entry initiative based on the premise that it can be easier and faster to gain market, product or technology access inorganically, via an M&A transaction, rather than building an organic capability internally. Having a clearly defined major strategic objective is important, Gisby emphasizes, "…because each goal can result in a different outcome, a different strategy, a different deal process and, for buyers, different targets." Keeping the overriding strategic objective in mind for quick and easy reference throughout the inevitable twists and turns of the deal process is key. For buyers, this ongoing reference point can help ensure that acquisition targets under consideration meet the strategic criteria. Gisby often reminds buyers of the difference between a candidate and an opportunity. "A candidate," Gisby says, "is an M&A target that on paper meets all or some of the buyer's pre-established strategic criteria; an opportunity, on the other hand, is a target that is actionable." He explains: "A buyer may be able to find a target candidate that meets all or some of those criteria. However, if that target is not prepared to engage in an M&A transaction then the discovery of that target by the buyer does not represent an opportunity."

Today, without a comprehensive M&A strategy, an acquisition can be a minefield.

"On the sell side," Gisby adds, "The process is similar, but reversed; the seller wants to identify the buyer's strategic objective. Is the buyer seeking to achieve a financial return or scale, or to leverage a seller's sales force, technology, markets or operations?" As with buyers, an M&A strategy provides the seller with a reality-based reference point during the M&A decision-making process when needed.

Scott Werry, Partner, Partners Group (a Toronto-based private equity firm that holds its portfolio companies for up to 12 years), provides a PE vantage point. "An M&A strategy is especially important in the hotly competitive contemporary private equity marketplace," Werry says, adding: "A well-conceived strategy enables us to proactively identify companies we admire and in which we want to invest – and a well-executed M&A strategy helps us close the deal."

For Andrew Lohmann, who chairs the M&A practice at Richmond, Virginia law firm Hirschler Fleisher, developing and adhering to an M&A strategy serves a self-protective purpose: "Valuations are so high now that unschooled buyers are vulnerable to overpayment."

Jeff Cox, Senior Partner, Mercer, leads the Chicago-based Mercer North American Private Equity M&A Group. "For buyers," Cox says, "today's multiples are so high that without a strategy and considerable discipline around core competency, buyers can encounter some unanticipated difficulty." For example, buyers can extend themselves into unfamiliar geographies that are rife with risk, such as the work councils in Germany, Italy and France. Says Cox, "We are involved in negotiating severance costs in order to shut down a factory in Italy. Those costs are enormous. Due to work council agreements, it is not uncommon for employers to pay a full year's wages to employees impacted by a plant closing. Multiply that and then take into account all other related costs, such as those associated with defined benefit plans. The price tag is very high."

Today, without a comprehensive M&A strategy, an acquisition can be a minefield, with unprepared buyers experiencing risk that they have never before encountered, and with no reference points as to how to manage it.

B. The Components of an M&A Strategy: To Each Its Own

"Every client is unique. Every situation is unique." – Brenen Hofstadter, President and Supervising Principal, Generational Capital Markets

There are no hard and fast components in a M&A strategy. The components differ according to the needs and aims of each buyer and seller. However, a well-developed M&A strategy offers a reliable roadmap for an organization's growth and translates a strategic business plan into a list of potential acquisition targets for buyers, or possible acquirers for sellers. The plan should also provide a framework for evaluating potential targets or buyers. The basic plan can consist of the following components:

- Translation of a company's strategic business plan into a set of drivers and requirements to be addressed by the M&A strategy. Drivers can include current and future markets; market share objectives; required products and needed technologies; current and future geographies; talent requirements; financial objectives; risk appetite and profile; competitor pre-emption assessment.

- For buyers, determination of acquisition financing constraints, including how the acquisition will be funded; the availability of surplus cash and credit facilities; the value of untapped and new equity as well as debt.

- A clear understanding of possible acquisition or sale pitfalls, including the criteria of the CFO, board of directors, investors and debt holders.

- A list of potential targets or acquirers and their profiles, including appropriate public stock and market research, competitor sections of public company 10K reports, employee recommendations, referrals from investment bankers, attorneys, board members and investors.

- For buyers, preliminary valuation models. For sellers, the desired valuation range.

- Target and acquirer candidates rated and ranked in terms of their impact on the buyer or seller's business and the feasibility of closing a transaction.

- A plan to review the M&A strategy with key stakeholders.

Brenen Hofstadter is President and Supervising Principal of Generational Capital Markets (GCM), a Dallas-based investment banking firm that specializes in representing privately held sellers – often family-owned businesses – mainly in North America. GCM deals typically occupy the $5 million-$500 million range. According to Hofstadter, from the seller perspective, especially if the seller is the owner and/or founder of a business, an M&A strategy should be based on seller understanding of the business and the likely buyers and the transaction's timing. "In truth," Hofstadter cautions, "The seller may have an understanding of one of those three pieces, but not all three." His firm's initial steps, he explains, "…include helping the seller understand a company's true value, the buyer universe, and what the ideal timing of the transaction ought to be. He, then, asks the seller to compare the company's value, the deal's prospective buyer universe, and the deal timing to the seller's personal and business goals to ensure alignment.

"Every client is unique; every situation is unique," Hofstadter says. "But all business owners who are seriously considering the sale of their company should answer the question: 'If the market timing is not a fit with my personal plans and goals, how do I continue to enhance value over time?' Often, sellers are cautious about moving into the M&A marketplace. In those instances, investment bankers can help enhance the company's value and scalability by maximizing deal flow within the tightest possible time frame via relationships with a wide range of deal brokers that specialize in a seller's industry and geography. Also helpful in this process are the use of Internet business listings, direct mail, direct phone calls, referrals from attorneys, accountants, bankers and other business owners, email campaigns and ads in trade journals."

Phillip Torrence is an attorney specializing in M&A, financial institutions and corporate governance at Honigman, Miller, Schwartz and Cohn, a Kalamazoo, Michigan law firm where he is also the Office Managing Partner. For buyers and sellers in M&A deals, he says, an M&A strategy helps set enterprise goals. "It's vital that buyers and sellers know why they are engaging in an M&A deal and what they hope to accomplish," he says. He recommends a narrowly constructed strategic focus to help ensure a successful transaction. An ill-conceived or more broadly focused M&A strategy, he notes, can result in a phenomenon Torrence regards as more common in M&A than casual observers realize: deal heat. Torrence defines deal heat as "doing a deal for the sake of doing a deal, which is often a recipe for disaster. Chasing and closing a deal can be a heady and thrilling experience for dealmakers. For buyers, a sound M&A strategy can point the way to a successful target digestion by the buyer."

From sellers, whether corporate, a family-owned business or a private equity firm, Torrence, assuming the perspective of a buyer, wants to be informed of seller objectives. He also recommends that sellers, with the aid of a law firm, conduct pre-deal self-diligence in order to make their companies even more attractive to potential buyers. "If it helps a seller obtain the desired sale price, self-diligence is well worth the expense," he declares.

According to Torrence, about 60 percent of his sell-side clients opt for self-diligence. "I help to sell many venture capital-backed companies, which means that we keep our corporate records and virtual data room current. In each venture capital financing, clients nearly replicate acquisition-related diligence, he says." Because of this experience, he says, his venture capital-backed clients are usually prepared for their eventual acquisition.

Attorney Andrew Lohmann (whose practice was named a "Law Firm of the Year" by The M&A Advisor in 2014) works mainly with entrepreneurial company founders/owners and private equity firms. He advocates identifying divisions of large companies and including them in an M&A strategy as candidates for prospective proprietary M&A transactions. Buyers prize such transactions, in which a specific buyer is awarded an opportunity to purchase a given division before that division is presented to other buyers by the parent company or by an investment banker. Getting that opportunity, however, requires aggressive buyer spadework, including diving deeply into contact networks to explore whether a desirable big-company subsidiary would be right for a carve-out.

"The 3-to-7-year non-compete and non-solicit provisions normally included in boilerplate M&A transaction purchase agreements or ancillary documents should perhaps also be re-imagined," Lohmann suggests. "There are opportunities for financial sellers to designate key individuals in the target company for retention as 'their' guys and attach a shorter non-solicitation term to such individuals. Traditionally, if a seller desires to be able to hire key employees of the target within a relatively short time after closing, it draws the buyer's ire. 'Heck, no,' the buyer says, 'Those people are key employees of the company we're buying!'"

Lohmann continues: "A way to resolve that issue early on is for the financial seller to include a short list of individuals as carve-outs to the normal non-solicitation term as a component in an M&A strategy."

He declares: "You don't get what you don't ask for," further advising that, "In addition to identifying synergies, a standard component in most buyer M&A strategies, a framework for conducting due diligence should also be included." In the diligence process, he says, strategic buyers tend to drill deeper on fewer issues.

"These issues," Lohmann points out, "may have burned them in past deals." Many financial buyers, on the other hand, conduct a broader diligence process, exploring every issue but perhaps not delving as deeply into issues that are more material. "What is needed…by today's strategic, financial and hybrid buyers is a more efficient diligence process streamlined for today's hyper-competitive M&A marketplace," he says.

DEAL NOTES

Speaking with…Savio Tung, Chief Investment Officer, Investcorp

The M&A Advisor visited with Savio Tung in his New York office. Savio is firm's Chief Investment Officer and also a founder of Investcorp, a provider and manager of alternative investment products, serving high net worth private and institutional clients. Investcorp, with $10.5 billion in assets under management, is active in five lines of business: Corporate investment in North America and Europe, corporate investment in technology, corporate investment in the Middle East and North Africa, real estate investment, and hedge funds. The M&A Advisor spoke with Tung about several issues, including the purpose and value of an M&A strategy, the relationship of M&A strategy with the auction process, the pros and cons of private equity involvement in M&A transaction, the realization of synergy opportunities and the avoidance of synergy pitfalls, and the importance of an international perspective.

On M&A strategy: "Reliance on gut instinct and macho does not work for me. I never proceed without a playbook. My vantage point is that of a middle market private equity investor. We are private equity buyers and sellers. We grow and nurture a company for 5-6 years and then harvest. A roll-up strategy is a key component of our investment thesis as it relates to private equity deals, because by creating synergies in one of our companies, or a strategic fit, or perhaps by strengthening a company's management team, we are enhancing the value of our investment. The result, for us, is a higher return on our investment.

"Although our middle market companies lack divisions to shed and reinvest capital into their core businesses, we have done many 'orphan transactions' in which we buy non-core divisions divested by larger companies. A business judged to be non-core by the parent then becomes a core business under our ownership. In a way, we are doing big corporations a favor by taking one of their divisions and focusing on its growth."

On how he competes with strategic buyers during the auction process: "The truth is that if a strategic buyer has perfect information, that buyer will win most auction processes. In our case, however, we are more efficient. We are more willing to commit to and mobile a team quickly. We also come across as more management-friendly. These are advantages we think can help us win versus a strategic buyer. However, strategic buyers sometimes have their own constraints because they must be concerned about management social issues, such as staff relocations, which can help neutralize their advantages over us. Sometimes strategic buyers complain that we are too 'cowboyish' and that we rush into decision-making. We, on the other hand, can argue that we do not miss the big picture. We, like strategic buyers, have a very good view of the forest, although we might miss a few of the trees."

On the pros and cons of private equity involvement in M&A transactions: "I am a dealmaker, not a middleman. I invest our limited partners' capital side by side with the management. I do this not for a fee, but to earn a return on investment. Having a PE partner in an M&A transaction means that the private equity partner has skin in the game. We tend to be more focused on management, and frankly, we do a better job in preparing our companies for sale. Although I won't claim that our companies are Sarbanes-Oxley compliant, they have engaged in the right initiatives and governance structures and thus are more ready for an IPO or to thrive as a private enterprise. Those are the pros. The two cons are: 1.) That we are not a long-term investor so are not proficient at making 10-year decisions, and, 2.) That we are not industry specialists. Therefore, we can't take over the operation of a company; we rely on the company's management to do that."

On promoting synergies early in the sales process: "If I were the seller I would promote the hell out of the synergies so that I can maximize the price. To the buyer, that represents risk. The margin of error is small. The buyer had better be right about being able to realize the synergy benefits. Any professor or consultant can follow a synergy plan and say, 'Combining these two companies will cut costs, generate revenue and we'll be able to lean on suppliers to obtain a bigger discount.' Those are easy to map out. But implementation and execution are another matter. I've never seen anyone who can execute precisely on a plan and on schedule. Slippage always exists, which is a big disadvantage to buyers."

On the synergy opportunities he seeks: "We have two companies. One company is more East Coast-centric. The other is West Coast-centric. When we combine the two companies, the sales forces do not overlap. There are no job losses. Overnight, we have a national footprint. We can tell customers that we can now provide nationwide services. That is synergy."

On avoiding synergy pitfalls: "Time and social issues are the two main impediments to synergy realization. Time is the biggest pitfall. We are always late. Everyone is always late. No one wants to be too drastic in pursuit of a schedule for fear of hurting the business. As for social issues, it is easy to map out a new organization chart, but telling each individual on that chart that he or she is staying or going is never a smooth process. I've seen executives below the CEO level balk at executing this phase because they are not accustomed to cutting off colleagues. Often, these conversations are fudged. We think we have exited an employee but instead that former employee returns to us as a consultant. This problem exists for strategic buyers and private equity alike."

On his international perspective: "Although we are a middle-market private equity business, our perspective has always had an international aspect. The following experience from the company's early years illustrates our continuing international perspective. In 1984, we purchased Tiffany from Avon. Tiffany annual sales were $4 million, most of which were generated in Japan. But Tiffany management assured us that it could grow the company, and we believed management. Two years later, revenues mushroomed to $145 million and today they exceed $1 billion. Does this mean that I am smarter than everyone else? No, it means that back in 1984 other private equity firms were US-focused, wanting to open stores in Phoenix, for example, while we envisioned stores in Hong Kong, Shanghai and Mexico City."

C. Aligning M&A Strategy with Corporate Strategy: Are They a Fit?

"Sometimes M&A strategy and corporate strategy fit, and sometimes they don't– but they should fit." – Jeff Cox, Senior Partner, North American Private Equity M&A Group, Mercer

Establishing an M&A strategy enables buyers and sellers to look through the windshield at the road ahead, rather than in the rear-view mirror at the past. In formulating an M&A strategy company strategists generate forward-looking questions and realistic responses. This exercise aids dealmakers in option evaluation. Usually, however, there are only two available options: accomplishing the stated objective internally and organically, or inorganically, by removing a competitor. A buyer that doesn't yet have a corporate strategy in place needs to construct one if a sizable M&A transaction is planned. Declares Phillip Torrence, "If a buyer is doing a deal that will grow the business by 25%, the buyer will be forced by that circumstance to closely analyze the direction of the company because the buyer will be doing all the modeling and determining the synergies that will enable the company to service its debt or, to the extent that the buyer is using cash off the balance sheet, to justify the returns on the money that is being put to work, as opposed to distributing those funds to shareholders."

"Sometimes M&A strategy and corporate strategy fit, and sometimes they don't–but they should fit," Jeff Cox remarks. With top line growth as the chief measure of a company's marketplace value, many companies need to grow, either organically or via acquisition. Companies that opt for an acquisition strategy need to know exactly what they are acquiring and why, counsels Cox. Do they want to expand a global footprint? Are they trying to grow a product line? How will the buyer's and seller's customers be impacted? Many companies are confronted by urgent considerations that demand a convergence of their M&A and corporate strategies. Companies have record cash on their corporate balance sheets and stock buy-backs are failing to supply needed lift. U.S.-domiciled multinationals have troves of cash parked outside the U.S. High U.S. taxes are the price for the repatriation of those cash hoards. Some tech companies are accepting the unknown risk inherent in investing in the emerging markets in which they carry cash on their balance sheets. The fact of the matter, says Cox, "is that M&A strategy and corporate strategy must fit in order for companies to experience any mid- to long-term success."

Investment bankers who represent sellers usually connect with prospective buyers that include M&A as part of their corporate strategy. Brenen Hofstadter is no exception. He analyzes the needs of buyers and sellers and attempts a match. Says Hofstadter, "Every transaction in which I've been involved during the past five years has included a buyer that was seeking to meet a specific need through M&A. For example," he explains, "Tarasoft Corp., the Canadian developer of the popular Matrix multiple listing service platform used by 17 North American MLS providers was acquired by CoreLogic, a real estate information and analytics provider, because the buyer desired the Tarasoft MLS technology, plus key managers and employees. Total Safety, a

"Every transaction in which I've been involved during the past five years has included a buyer who was seeking to meet a specific need through M&A." ~ Brenen Hofstadter

global provider of integrated safety solutions, acquired Pacific Environmental Consulting, a western Canada-based occupational safety and consulting firm, in order to facilitate geographic expansion into western Canada. The recent acquisition of Johnston Grain, Oklahoma's oldest and largest privately owned grain company, by CGB Enterprises, a US company with Japanese parentage, provided Johnston, the seller, with access to the buyer's global grain markets."

According to attorney Frank Koranda, Jr., a Shareholder at Polsinelli, M&A is usually the growth-through-acquisition component of corporate strategy, but a corporate strategy would also include strategic alliances and human resources initiatives that are unrelated to M&A. Yet, in family offices – law firms that cater to families with a net worth of $50 million-$100 million that have recently experienced a wealth creation event like the sale of a family-owned, privately held company – he has witnessed instances in which an M&A strategy can actually directly engender a corporate strategy by efficiently deploying available capital for acquisitions and related investments.

Yet if no overall corporate strategy exists, can the development of an M&A strategy also result in the creation of a corporate strategy? Cox and Koranda believe the answer is yes. Cox has seen instances where traditionally non-acquisitive companies have cut an M&A deal. He cites a recent transaction in which the buyer, with an aging work force "on the back nine" acquired a company that not only provided the acquirer with an expanded product line but also with vigorous senior managers who eventually proved to be more capable than the buyer's incumbent managers in expanding the buyer's global footprint. According to Koranda, the buyer CEO said, "'I don't think we have senior managers that are the best of the best. In the new company, however, I want the best of the best.'" Explains Koranda: "We did competency modeling for attributes the CEO wanted for her senior leadership team. We traveled around the world to interview leaders from the buyer and the target. Today, the new company's executive team consists mainly of managers who transitioned from the target."

Deloitte's Simon Gisby sees a potential danger in creating a corporate strategy based on an M&A strategy because then there is a risk that a company will pursue M&A purely for the sake of pursuing M&A. "The result," he cautions, "can be a company afflicted with 'dealitis', where transaction pursuit supersedes strategy, thus creating a cycle of poor decision-making."

In short, a corporate strategy is a must in order to prioritize specific short- and long-term company goals and to outline the organization's direction at the board of directors, executive management and ownership levels. M&A, whether it involves a proactive decision not to execute M&A transactions, or to move ahead aggressively, is a crucial aspect of corporate strategy, one that can be revisited and refocused to adapt to changing corporate needs or marketplace realities.

D. How to Avoid Auction Process Pitfalls: Stick to Strategy

"It's like a high-wire act at the circus; everything appears to be going smoothly, and then..." – Phillip Torrence, Leader/Financial Institutions and Corporate Governance Groups, Honigman, Miller, Schwartz & Cohn

The scenario is too familiar to many dealmakers: a transaction begins in the usual fashion, with buyer and seller adhering to their respective strategic playbooks while seeking to obtain optimum terms. The deal moves ahead. Then the jockeying between buyer and seller accelerates as a definitive agreement comes into view. Now the adrenaline spurts and one or both of the parties begins to lose a grip on their strategic moorings. Emotion sometimes trumps logic. Decision-making is impacted. One observer likens this phase to the scene in the movie Jaws, when two fishermen imprudently heave a hook baited with a roast beef from a dock at night in an attempt to lure the giant great white shark into shore. The big shark takes the beef-baited hook and aims for open water, pulling the entire dock into the water and taking dock and thrashing fishermen for a ride for which they had not planned and for which they had failed to prepare. In such instances in the course of an M&A transaction, several unintended consequences can result, none of them beneficial to both parties: the buyer overpays for the target; caught up in the heat of the moment, the buyer is unable to capture the planned deal model synergies. In the worst case, the deal, like the doomed luxury liner Titanic in the 1997 film of the same name, breaks asunder, with buyer and seller taking a bracing ice bath.

Avoiding adrenaline-fueled deal pitfalls is easier said than done, but they can, and have been avoided. Phil Torrence says that he cautions buyer and seller clients about the precarious nature of the deal execution process. "I advise them that it's like a high-wire act at the circus; everything appears to going smoothly, and then…" A single misstep or emotion-based misjudgment, when buyer or seller veers from their respective strategic foundations, can topple a carefully constructed deal or result in a transaction that will ultimately prove to be unsuccessful for either, or both, parties.

"In some cases," says Torrence, "the presence of multiple prospective buyers in the phase leading up to the definitive agreement is healthy for buyers and sellers alike." Often, however, in the frenzy of the moment, a buyer push for exclusivity can induce that buyer to grossly overpay. "In such situations," Torrence says, "I'm reminded of my college economics professor who often cautioned against impulsive decision-making by using the acronym, TANSTAAFL – There Ain't No Such Thing as a Free Lunch. Occasionally, a buyer bid that far exceeds the others is too good to be true. Sellers must be careful when considering exclusivity: If the seller opts for exclusivity the purchase is re-traded several times until it drops below competing bids." Sellers, of course, can elect to let the exclusivity period run its course and then reenter the marketplace. "But then they are seen as damaged goods," Torrence remarks.

Competitive juices often begin to flow during the diligence process, when emotions can be brought into play. "Giving into those competitive urges," says Frank Koranda, "must be avoided at all costs." Decision-making should be cool and unemotional. According to Koranda, the only relevant decision for buyers is, "Do you want to buy the asset at a certain price?" Especially for corporate buyers, that decision is very strategic.

Says Koranda: "So whether the buyer pays a dollar more than anticipated may not have huge implications if the buyer takes a medium- or long-term view of the target's prospects and potential synergistic fit. Maintaining a disciplined decision-making posture and perspective requires an M&A strategy that is closely aligned with corporate strategy. That perspective," he adds, "should be refined well in advance of an auction."

For buyers, remaining true to their investment thesis is one near-surefire way to avoid the dangers of deal heat, deal-itis or auction frenzy. Says attorney

Andrew Lohmann, "I know of private equity firms that did not make a single acquisition for a year or two because they chose to remain true to their investment thesis. Nevertheless," he adds, "in overheated environments, like the current M&A marketplace, in which private equity firms possess plentiful 'dry powder' and are active in raising new funds, it is difficult not to be caught up in the action and perhaps stretching too far in an attempt to do a deal.

"There is a fine line between being creative, diving deeply to find synergies to justify a transaction, and trying to justify an acquisition because there needs to be some activity that's visible to the limited partners," Lohmann comments. Patience, however, and sticking with investment thesis principles, can win the day for buyers and sellers looking to circumvent the potential dangers of auction frenzy.

However, a limited auction is not a potential pitfall to Brenen Hofstadter, who represents sellers. In fact, his firm is a proponent of the limited auction concept. He uses that process to sift through buyers in order to find those that are the most serious in terms of their capacity to create the best synergies for his seller clients. "Buyers," Hofstadter asserts, "try to weigh the value of paying a premium, a perceived premium or a slight premium through the auction process as opposed to a direct deal through a exclusive arrangement. Some buyers are more effective at that than others," he notes. "Getting the attention of the owners of privately held businesses can be difficult," he says, "as is creating deal flow for the buyer universe." Educating and escorting a seller through the pitfalls of the auction process is a necessity, Hofstadter says: "For most owners, one auction process is all they will experience during their lifetimes."

Today, thanks to the widening imbalance between deal supply and demand, the normal auction process, always an enervating experience for buyers and sellers, has become even more intense. Explains Jeff Cox, "From start to finish, the auction process is far more abbreviated compared to a year ago." Private equity money is time-limited and must be spent. Multiples are skyrocketing: Berkshire Hathaway paid 15X earnings for Chicago's Portillo's Restaurant Group in July 2014. "Portillo's is very profitable," says Cox, "but the expectation is that consumers worldwide will eat hot dogs at the same rate as Chicagoans in order for the buyer to earn a satisfactory ROI. The tipping point was the $2 billion sale of the Los Angeles Dodgers baseball team headed by the

Guggenheim Partners' hedge fund, which was backed by insurance company investors. The Dodgers investors expect a 4.6 percent ROI."

From his vantage point at Mercer, Cox says that he "sees some of the big players now reaching down into the middle market." He sees buyers that have traditionally purchased in-country assets only in Canada, for example, is now seeking US assets and acquirers that had limited themselves to acquiring North American assets now exploring acquisition opportunities in Central Europe. "It's all over the board," Cox declares. "Deal demand is high because hedge funds and activist investors are in the face of corporate America, which is sitting on an unprecedented cash hoard with nowhere to spend it."

In addition, private equity funds are obligated to invest time-limited money. Exits and initial public offerings are at all-time highs thanks to sky-high multiples. Stock buybacks are no longer efficient. Therefore, corporations must accept additional risk. Says Cox, "Wall Street is rewarding corporations' top-line growth, but they can't grow organically, they have to buy." The result, for some companies and investors, is a level of risk many have not previously experienced.

There is often a tendency for some dealmakers to become so wrapped in the auction process "that they lose their ability to see the woods for the trees," says Simon Gisby. "Decision-making flaws exposed in the throes of emotional responses cannot be camouflaged by documentation," he points out. "You can never document yourself out of a bad deal," he emphasizes, saying that any M&A strategy should have checkpoints placed throughout the process or a framework that enables dealmakers to constantly assess the decision-making process to ascertain that the M&A strategic objectives are being achieved. If the objectives become lost in an auction process gone awry, a strategic framework provides the dealmakers with the opportunity to either modify the deal or walk away from it. "A buyer or seller declaration that [says] 'I've got to close this deal at all costs' could be a recipe for an M&A failure," says Gisby.

E. Using an M&A Strategy to Identify Non-Core Investment Disposal and Spin-Offs

"There are probably portfolios within an acquired company that need to be scrutinized because they are not core to the buyer's business." – Cathy Skala, Vice President/Integration, Baxter International, Inc.

The M&A landscape is rife with evidence that failures of synergy are compelling enterprises to shed businesses that once were a tight fit with corporate strategy but now are not. Corporate and M&A strategies in industry clusters such as media and broadcast, for example, now call for the rending of internal strategic ties that have been in place for generations. Chicago's Tribune Company has spun off the print version of the venerable Chicago Tribune. Time Warner has spun off all of its iconic print stalwarts, including Fortune, Money, Sports Illustrated and Time Magazine itself. E.W. Scripps and Journal Communications, publishers of the Milwaukee Sentinel newspaper and other print properties, announced in mid-summer 2014 that they planned to merge and then spin off their combined slower-growing newspapers, leaving the merged entity focused on broadcast television.

The transaction will create two publicly traded companies. One, which would retain the E.W. Scripps corporate moniker, would be one of the largest owners of ABC-affiliated TV stations, with a presence in eight states, including Florida, Texas, Colorado, Missouri and Ohio. The other corporate entity, dubbed the Journal Media Group, will own newspapers in 14 markets and is expected to generate more than $800 million in annual revenues. Gannett, the owner of the national newspaper USA Today, will also split its print and non-print businesses, spinning off its print properties, including USA Today, into a separate publicly traded company.

"This trend," says Phillip Torrence, "has been incubating for the past two decades as once-lush print businesses were steadily outflanked by digital media. 2.0 of this trend will likely find flush social media companies like Facebook and Twitter acquiring big newspaper publishers. The fit is a natural." Other industries, including healthcare, are undergoing a similar transition.

Adhering to an M&A strategy has resulted in subsidiary spin-offs at other large corporations, such as Tyco and Johnson & Johnson. Procter & Gamble, traditionally among the Midwest's highest-profile corporations, has yet to set a definitive course regarding M&A, Jeff Cox notes: "P&G invited a hedge fund to analyze its corporate structure; the hedge fund recommended that the entire company be broken up." Procter & Gamble senior management determined that it aspired to achieve a number one or one-and-a-half ranking in every market category in which the company was to remain active. "P&G looked at the categories in which the company was ranked third or fourth and decided that buying its way to the top ranking did not make sense," Cox says.

In those categories – with one exception in which P&G decided it could buy the top ranking – an exit strategy was deemed appropriate. As companies sort through acquisition opportunities in search of those that are most appropriate according to their M&A strategy, most will likely conduct an exhaustive review to learn which target will bring them the most substantial ROI.

All companies, large and middle market, can benefit from employing their M&A strategy to identify parts of their businesses that are candidates for divestiture because those assets are not aligned with M&A or corporate strategy. Acquisition targets can be scrutinized in the same fashion, according to Cathy Skala, Vice President/Integration at Baxter International, Inc., a Chicago-area healthcare company that focuses on products to treat hemophilia, kidney disease, immune disorders and other chronic and acute medical conditions. "There are probably portfolios within any given acquisition that need to be scrutinized because they are not core to the buyer's business," Skala says. "It's important that the targets housing those units not be screened out, but the eventual buyer should be purposeful in ensuring that non-core business units of groups are spun off as soon as practicable in order for the acquirer to remain true to its core and to its corporate strategy."

"An M&A strategy can certainly apply to the buy side of a transaction," says Scott Werry, ""f the buyer is aiming to grow a business via M&A." He recommends that buyers continually refine, reshape and refocus their businesses around core priorities. Simon Gisby counsels that an M&A strategy should not focus purely on external M&A but also on internal M&A in the form of portfolio realignment. "For example," he says, "if the goal of M&A is financially driven, a question should be asked. Can the financial objective achieved via a company's existing portfolio of products, services, geographies or businesses rather than seeking M&A opportunities? The M&A lens should be focused internally and externally," Gisby says.

Part II: Private Equity Involvement in M&A: Pros and Cons

A. Private Equity's Evolving Role: What's Old Is New Again

"Private equity is beginning to again outpace and outpay strategics." – Phillip Torrence, Leader, Financial Institutions and Corporate Governance Groups, Honigman, Miller, Schwartz & Cohn

Just a few years ago, private equity firms ruled the M&A roost. Deals were plentiful as were eager limited partners. Then came the global recession. Fast-forward to 2014 and a slowly recovering economy. Deals are not yet as plentiful as they once were. Those that exist attract a long list of buyer candidates, many of which are well-heeled corporate strategics. Although they compete aggressively with strategics for deals, many private equity firms only rarely find themselves in the buyer winner's circle. The reason: Strategics, for the moment, are often all too willing and able to wildly outspend their private equity competitors in pursuit of a valued target. Yet there are strong signs that private equity firms are beginning to rebalance the competitive deal environment in their favor. Declares attorney Phillip Torrence, "Private equity is beginning to again outpace strategics. Torrence recalls that, prior to 2008, "…Strategics would put their checkbooks away when private equity entered the auction process, because private equity firms were usually willing to pay so much more." After the recession hit, private equity firms, thanks to banks' borrowing limitations, lost the leverage that had produced such attractive returns to investors. Beginning in 2012, however, the pendulum began to swing in favor of private equity. Although strategics continue to hold sway in an overheated deal environment, private equity is back in the hunt.

Nevertheless, PE firms continue to hang back as buyers, kept at bay as the lure of strong equity markets convinces funds seeking to exit assets to opt for a public share sale or to turn to cash-laden corporate buyers. Most PE firms, however, are wrestling with asset price inflation as valuations, fueled in part by asset scarcity, the swing to IPOs as well as a growing volume of undeployed fund capital leaves PE firms paying out more as they seek ways to spend cash. Multiples have risen steeply and PE firms continue to slowly but steadily acclimatize to steeper purchase prices.

B. The Pros

"Private equity firms can be relied on to provide a floor on valuation and to skillfully execute a transaction." – Scott Werry, Partner, Altas Partners

Astute financial buyers with management and operating capabilities, private equity firms mostly share a common business model: They buy, develop and subsequently sell businesses. They acquire operating companies for their fund's portfolio by making direct equity investments into those portfolio companies in exchange for a percentage of ownership. Most PE targets have already matured beyond the proof-of-concept phase, with targets possessing a definable market position, a solid revenue base, sustainable cash flow and a competitive advantage plus the opportunity for further growth and expansion. PE buyers expect to profit from the cash flow thrown off by the operating company and from capital gains on exit. Most PE firms share an incubation period of five to seven years for each portfolio company before the company's sale. The exit provides a private equity firm with liquidity that can then be used to invest in another portfolio company or to distribute as proceeds to the firm's limited partners.

On the plus side, PE firms can provide portfolio companies with large funding infusions often measured in hundreds of millions to billions of dollars. In numerous instances, these funding infusions can spur portfolio company growth, thereby igniting hiring. PE firms are active managers of their portfolio companies, finding ways to maximize value. Many PE firms prefer to retain portfolio company senior executives in whom they have confidence and then provide them with the means to grow the company and prepare it for sale. The combination of bountiful funding, expertise and various incentives can bring positive results for investors in PE funds and for retained portfolio company managers. In fact, a 2012 Boston Consulting Group survey found that more than two-thirds of PE transactions resulted in at least a 20% growth in portfolio company profits, and about half the deals generated portfolio company profit growth of at least 50%.

"PE firms can be relied on to provide a floor for valuation and to execute a transaction," Scott Werry points out. "These two benefits," he adds, "provide sellers with a price to compare with other alternatives, such as an IPO or a sale to a corporate buyer. For corporate buyers," he says, "there can be a benefit to partnering with a private equity firm. PE firms are able to bring execution capabilities to the transaction process, especially during the due diligence phase. PE firms can work with a corporate buyer throughout the deal process, capitalizing on their efficient execution to close a deal."

Attorney Frank Koranda works with middle market buyers and sellers and is familiar with the transactional skill of PE firms in an M&A deal. "PE firms," he insists, "can react more rapidly to opportunities than strategics that are often burdened by sizable bureaucracies. For sellers," he adds, "the number of PE firms and the diversity of the PE universe often represent more options for sellers. Sellers can parse that PE universe to find the firm with most appropriate experience in the seller's space," Koranda says.

"For buyers," says Andrew Lohmann, "involvement with a PE firm means access to capital." For lower middle market sellers hoping to retain their senior managers after an acquisition, there are PE firms that take a non-control approach or assume a position as a mezzanine lender. Another advantage for sellers in using a PE firm, according to Simon Gisby, is that PE firms adhere to the seller's timetable as well as provide competitive tension throughout the sale process. "For strategic buyers," Lohmann says, "the major attraction of PE firms is their ability to respond to 'big deadlines.'"

Brenen Hofstadter, in representing lower-middle-market and middle-market sellers almost exclusively, likes to include private equity firms on the roster of prospective buyers. He prefers PE firms that have holdings in his clients' marketplace space. "There are thousands of PE firms operating in North America and we have access to many of them through our databases and our relationships, but we focus on the top 50 that operate in our client's space." Hofstadter says.

In the current overheated and often overpriced deal environment, there is an emerging way for strategics and PE firms to collaborate for the benefit of both. When a large multinational decides to shed subsidiaries, prospective middle market strategic buyers that want just a slice of the subsidiary to complement their business often find themselves trampled by a stampede of big strategics willing and able to swallow the entire sub. According to Jeff Cox, this scenario represents a perfect moment for PE firms to partner with some of the wealthier middle market buyers on non-core assets that the strategic does not wish to buy in their entirety. The middle market buyer can buy the entire subsidiary, scoop out the slice of the business it wants and private equity can take the remainder. Explains Cox, "This will enable the middle market buyer with a healthy balance sheet to be successful in a bid without assuming excessive risk." As an example, he cites a cross-border deal in which he was involved. His client was a US-based beverage company that wanted the beverage division of a food company in a former Communist-bloc country. Although his client might have partnered with a PE firm to strike a deal, it chose not to do so. Nevertheless, the model is valid, Cox insists. "The objective for a middle market strategic," he says, "is to find a PE buyer with a similar culture that possesses the necessary discipline and rigor and is prepared to make the needed investments." With plentiful funding available for strong deals, PE firms like Toronto's Altas Partners choose to access deal financing after a transaction is arranged rather than raising a fund. Jeff Cox calls this concept "another very intriguing investment model."

Some sellers opt for exclusive arrangements with private equity firms to achieve marketplace leverage by not exposing their sale strategy to competitors. "The information will eventually reach the marketplace, even with non-disclosure agreements," says Phillip Torrence, "but using exclusivity with a PE firm to prolong secrecy has been proven to be an effective tactic. For buyers, teaming with a private equity firm provides a link to the deep knowledge base possessed by some PE firms."

C. The Cons

"When a private equity firm enters the picture, there is a new sheriff in town." - Frank Koranda, Jr., Shareholder, Polsinelli

For some sellers, the dilution of their ownership position, thanks to a relationship with a PE firm, may prove to be a negative. Association with a private equity group provides buyers with plentiful funding but can also, in some cases, result in the loss of control of basic elements of business operation, such as strategy formulation, employee hiring and dismissal and management team selection. Other acquisition financing options can also involve relinquishing of seller control, but because a PE firm's stake in a target is usually higher than a strategic's, the chance for seller loss of control is sometimes greater. Loss of decision-making control can impact the exit strategy for a PE portfolio company, which may involve an outright sale that might not have been the chosen strategy of the portfolio company's management team. As financial buyers whose prime objective is to enhance the value of a portfolio company for sale purposes to maximize sale profits, the perspective of private equity firms can sometimes conflict with the approach of target company owner/managers who may possess a broader outlook and who, in some instances, may place a higher premium on employee and customer relationships and corporate reputational issues than a PE owner might.

Post-close job security is often a concern for a target's key managers. "Some are happy to ride off into the sunset," says Andrew Lohmann, "but most want to stay on and perhaps obtain stock options or synthetic equity, thus getting a second bite of the apple five years down the road." Another potential negative associated with private equity involvement in M&A deals is that fewer cost and revenue synergies may exist than were hoped for by the seller. "Maybe there is less likelihood of achieving an optimal purchase price from a private equity buyer than from a quasi-strategic buyer with a financial objective but a synergistic platform," remarks Lohmann.

In addition to a lower-than-anticipated valuation, a potential cultural change can represent a private equity negative to some sellers. Frank Koranda frequently works with middle market sellers. He says, "What I often see is that when a PE firm enters, there is a new sheriff in town." PE firms can impose new metrics and deliverables on sellers, he adds: "When considering the impact of a private equity buyer on their organization, members of a seller senior management team ought to be aware that when the transaction closes the PE buyer may also impose a cultural change on the acquired company." The question of whether senior managers will be comfortable with such a change needs to be resolved by those managers who decide to remain with the post-acquisition company.

DEAL NOTES

Planning for Synergy Realization: Do It Early

Developing a formula for calculating synergy realization is a must-do post-close task. Failure to undertake these calculations is likely to have a disastrous impact on the chances for a transaction's long-term success. Simon Gisby, Managing Director, Deloitte Corporate Finance LLC, puts it clearly: establish a day-one readiness plan post-close. "At some point between the LOI and the close, maybe even pre-LOI, best practice is for the buyer to begin mapping out post-close integration in the classic day 1-100 timeframe." Depending on the nature of the transaction and how the deal is negotiated, it may be possible for the synergy realization mapping to start pre-close with the collaboration of the seller. Gisby advises: "Buyers should never place themselves in a position where they are closing a deal minus any plan to realize anticipated synergies. Sellers are caught in a balancing act: though there is a need to collaborate with buyers in an early forward planning effort, they have to balance that need against the possibility that the planning process may disrupt their business, or that the deal may not be consummated." He emphasizes that "the early formulation of a plan to realize synergies is a necessity for both parties in the transaction."

Cathy Skala, Vice President/Integration, Baxter International, Inc., advocates a close examination of the target's finances and cost structure. Such an examination, based on benchmarks, should enable the buyer to gain an understanding of the cost of the target's goods sold, the rough general and administrative expense and R&D. "Buyers should look at the percentages and compare them to their own costs in those areas," she advises. "If the buyer sees marked disparities from typically expected costs, that is a red flag."

For attorney Phillip Torrence, Office Managing Partner at Kalamazoo, Michigan law firm Honigman, Miller, Schwartz & Cohn, red flags in the synergy planning process have a human face. "These individuals exist in every organization," he says, "and either resist the planning process or prefer to favor assumptions rather than calculations." He cautions his clients with this advice: "You can't do a good deal with a bad guy." However, buyer/seller collaboration represents a bright green light for Torrence. "The most fruitful scenario," he says, "is one in which buyer and seller management team members do discuss their current businesses but engage real-time in collaboration about the direction of their industry."

Jeff Cox, Senior Partner, North American Private Equity M&A Group, Mercer, is faced with the task of effecting timely resolution of synergy-related HR issues covering myriad categories, including change control and retention agreements, severance and enhanced severance and the transfer of assets related to assuming control over defined benefit or 401(k) plans. Then there is the potentially thorny calculation of reserves available for active medical claims. "If we anticipate inheriting an ongoing real-time liability, that liability must be estimated on a go-forward basis to protect the buyer. It's a challenge."

Jeff Cox, Senior Partner, North American Private Equity M&A Group, Mercer, is faced with the task of effecting timely resolution of synergy-related HR issues covering myriad categories, including change control and retention agreements, severance and enhanced severance and the transfer of assets related to assuming control over defined benefit or 401(k) plans. Then there is the potentially thorny calculation of reserves available for active medical claims. "If we anticipate inheriting an ongoing real-time liability, that liability must be estimated on a go-forward basis to protect the buyer. It's a challenge."

Part III: Synergy Identification and Calculation: the End of the Beginning

A. Including Synergy Opportunities in an M&A Strategy

"It all depends on the deal and why the deal is being done." – Cathy Skala, Vice President/Integration, Baxter International

When buyers pay for synergies in M&A transactions that are based on goals set for in their M&A strategies, they are paying for synergy opportunities, not for the certainty that those opportunities can be realized, which is a separate challenge for buyers. Many deals feature significant opportunities for creating incremental cash flows from cost reductions and gains in revenue. In most deals, buyers succeed in gleaning synergistic value from low-hanging fruit – job redundancies and consolidation of real estate, for example – but some buyers are not as effective at identifying, valuing and capturing synergies that are less defined, such as revenue-related synergies or synergies gained from skills transfers. Revenue synergies can prove to be especially difficult to value and capture and are frequently overvalued. Some dealmakers suggest that revenue synergies should not be included in the deal valuation process. Some insist that such synergies are non-existent, although most dealmakers consider revenue to be a source of real value. In any case, the match of M&A strategy to synergy realization is sometimes based on assumptions and calculations that may not play out as anticipated in the long run. The key is to use M&A strategy as a framework for synergy identification and appraisal, and to proceed cautiously in identifying and calculating synergies that are likely to be real and lasting, culling out those that are likely to be aspirational only.

Private equity firms that are creating M&A strategies are likely to find synergies in a target's finance department, back office IT support and perhaps a geographic overlap in sales teams, depending on the target's existing platform, according to Frank Koranda. PE-acquired companies that are not roll-ups, however, may lack a roll-up's support platform and thus will require assistance from the PE sponsor to build one; in most cases, a platform will need to be built organically. "In strategic deals, however," Koranda adds, "synergies may be quickly achieved because the buyer platform already exists."

On the revenue side, PE firm executive Scott Werry says his M&A strategy seeks ways to cross-sell products or services to new customers and channels. On the cost side, this M&A strategy plots synergies to be gained, although he admits this strategy is difficult to execute. In the production of goods and services, cost-saving synergies could include selling, general and administrative expenses (SG&A), and ways to purchase items in bulk to achieve procurement savings, as well as resolving redundancies in employment, services and manufacturing.

Seller rep Brenon Hofstadter looks to buyers from the seller's industry to provide new customer markets, or specific products and services that complement the seller's offerings. Echoing Frank Koranda, Hostadter looks to

"Seller finance and accounting systems represent the first changes a strategic buyer makes post-close." ~ *Brenen Hofstadter*

---

buyers to also provide finance and accounting systems that are sophisticated than his client's. In fact, he adds, "Seller finance and accounting systems represent [those] first changes a strategic buyer makes post-close." He says that this strategy "calls for a prospective buyer to also bring a sophisticated board of directors, and the capability to execute add-on acquisitions, both of which my client usually lacks."

"Synergy realization hinges on the M&A strategy," declares Cathy Skala. "It all depends on the deal [and] why the deal is being done." In deals that are focused on achieving revenue synergies, for example, the emphasis is on developing, cross-referral and cross-sell capabilities and/or entering new geographies. "In deals focused on revenue synergies," Skala explains, "cost synergies are secondary: they are there but they are not the main focus of the deal." However, other transactions are more focused on cost synergies, "because the buyer is not only expanding its portfolio but also seeking to capture more margin," Skala says. Cost synergies are then found in eliminating redundancies associated with back-office functions. In the revenue-focused deals consummated by her company, Baxter International, achieving supply chain synergies has been a primary driver, as have purchasing synergies on the cost side, adds Skala.

Talent acquisition synergies have been the chief strategic objective in the deals in which Phillip Torrence has been a participant. "Many dealmakers concentrate on the so-called 'hard' revenue and cost synergies," Torrence points out, "but it is the top-third level of vice presidents who have a deep understanding of a business that his clients seek to 'lock up' in the transaction. They're the ones I like my teams to focus on first, before they address the hard assets." Torrence also uses the deal process to have his team members in-depth interview with key target managers.

Simon Gisby takes the more traditional route, favoring growth-oriented revenue synergies that facilitate the following: Penetration of new markets; cross-selling; leveraging special property and technology to create new customers and enter new geographies; leveraging operating costs in manufacturing, supply chain, distribution and IT; leveraging alternative access to capital, including less expensive capital; and leveraging vendor costs. Sellers, he says, should look down their entire P&L, line by line, to pinpoint synergistic opportunities. "The reason for such a seller review," Gisby says, "is that this is the exact analysis that the buyer is conducting. All of this connects with the objectives set forth in the buyer's M&A strategy and with the need for that strategy." Does the target enable the buyer to meet the M&A strategy's revenue-related objectives? Is the acquirer able to generate increased revenues from the same cost base or from a lower cost base? "On the balance sheet," Gisby says, "the issues usually hinge on capital costs and the likelihood that working capital can be improved."

Human resources-related synergies are Jeff Cox's specialty, "because the synergy opportunities in that space are huge," he declares. He seeks answers to the following questions: What is the buyer or seller's risk tolerance? Which seller best practices, observed by the buyer during diligence, match up with the buyer? "We look at anything and everything around HR-related practices, such as employee awards, how the seller drives employee behaviors, communications policies, infrastructure configuration, training and development, talent management and succession training," Cox states.

B. Early Promotion of Potential Synergies: What Are the Disadvantages for Buyers?

"Know your audience." - Frank Koranda, Shareholder, Polsinelli

Synergy promotion by buyers and sellers can be a slippery slope for both. There are clear advantages for each if their promotion tactics succeed, but also dangers in that a buyer may pay too much for too little and a seller may sell too much for too little.

When it comes to early promotion of synergies by buyers, is modesty, or honesty, the best policy? According to Andrew Lohmann, buyer restraint is usually advisable: "A buyer touting synergies, and how the enterprise will be bolstered by acquisitions, can seem threatening to sellers who may hear in that expressed vision the strong hint of consolidation and the possible elimination of certain positions, including those of the seller CEO and members of the seller management team."

Another possible pitfall for sellers when a potential buyer extols synergy is the occasional tendency of some seller investment bankers to try to capitalize on buyer optimism by exaggerating the potential synergies to convince the buyer to increase the purchase price beyond that cited in the initial indication of interest. The unintended result for sellers is that the buyer then downplays the potential synergies in order to lower the price. On the flipside, buyers may gain an advantage because early synergy touting captures seller interest and may differentiate the buyer from the competition.

Over-eager sellers are also capable of touting potential synergies. "Every seller number I see is pro forma-adjusted, which begs the question, if sellers are promoting potential synergies, why didn't the sellers achieve those synergies on their own?" says Jeff Cox. The disadvantage for the buyer who takes the seller's synergy bait and opts for the acquisition is that the potential synergies may ultimately prove to be little more than smoke and mirrors. A fail-safe solution: It is incumbent upon the buyer and seller to do their own diligence.

The advantage for the seller in promoting potential synergies is that such promotion demonstrates and illustrates the value creation the transaction will have for a buyer and, by doing so, position the seller to negotiate some of that value creation. According to Simon Gisby, "The intrinsic value of the target as a stand-alone, by definition, should be less than the intrinsic value of that business for the buyer." The difference between the two is the value creation the buyer expects to garner from the acquisition, which is the ROI of the transaction. For the seller, the art of the deal is to capture, in the sale price, much of that intrinsic value. One way for the seller to achieve that objective is to illustrate for the buyer the synergies the buyer will likely obtain from the deal, therefore implying to the buyer that the seller is unwilling to sell for the company's stand-alone intrinsic value but expects to share in the benefit the buyer will derive from the transaction. For sellers, explains Gisby, "This often means engaging in a different synergy analysis for each potential buyer. The buyer, however, does not appreciate being sent an analysis by the seller." Instead, he says, the buyer prefers to create its own synergy analysis and, to the extent possible, keep the results of that analysis proprietary so that the seller remains unaware of the potential value creation the buyer anticipates to derive from the deal. The buyer will always prefer to pay the stand-alone value of the target, while the seller wants to be paid as much as possible of the intrinsic value the buyer expects. "The art," declares Gisby, "is in how the difference is split."

To Cathy Skala, this art form represents a tricky balance for both buyers and sellers. "The seller obviously desires a sale," she says, "but may be promoting synergies based on the seller's parochial perception, whereas the buyer's perception of those synergies may differ according to how the buyer is organized and structured. If the buyer is not well-educated in how to assess a deal, the buyer is susceptible to being oversold by the seller on potential synergies, synergies that cannot be realized because those touted by the seller fail to align with the buyer's organization." To Skala, the buyer should take its own realistic assessment of potential synergies, consider the seller's assessment, but not accept the seller assessment as gospel.

Brenen Hofstadter coaches his seller clients to promote synergies by offering memos during buyer visits to pique buyer interest and hopefully to maximize value. Yet he also counsels sellers to avoid over-promising. Business owners tend toward optimism regarding synergies and the potential of the business they have built, especially should their business become aligned with a larger corporate entity, Hofstadter points out. "However," he adds, "the most astute buyers I've worked with during 100-plus M&A transactions are those that bring other aspects to the table in addition to money." For example, a buyer from the seller's industry will bring new customer markets, a product or service that might dovetail with the seller's offerings, plus financial and accounting systems that are more sophisticated and efficient than the seller's. "Sellers can indeed oversell synergies," Frank Koranda says, "a tactic that may cost sellers dearly in the near future. Rather than emphasizing pricing, it is better to identify the areas in the seller company that might fit comfortably into buyer organizations." Koranda's advice: "Know your audience; customize the presentation to fit that audience."

C. Avoiding Synergy-Related Pitfalls: Early Identification Is Vital

"You have to give yourself truth serum when you ask yourself, can I really do this in the designated time period?" – Simon Gisby, Managing Director, Deloitte Corporate Finance

It often seems that there are as many synergy pitfalls and the ways to avoid them as there are dealmakers. What there is, though, are two universally accepted words of advice regarding synergy realization pitfalls: early identification. Employing those words of advice, however, can be trying in the days following a deal closing. Fatigue hangs heavy, flavored by the dregs of a fast-fading adrenaline rush. A breather is needed by all the deal participants. But this is no time for a breather. Deal decompression is but a cruel mirage. Deal fatigue, to Frank Koranda, looms as the major impediment to early identification of synergy-related pitfalls. "Renewed energy is needed as soon as the closing ink dries, but there is precious little immediately available to negotiate the challenges of the ensuing 100 days, the usual time frame for dealmakers to claim a captive audience. Employees are ready. They may never be more attentive. They are open to change and malleable. According to Koranda, the most effective way for dealmakers to cope with deal fatigue while still moving forward to synergy realization is for a transition team to begin working and planning in earnest to cope with potential pitfalls while the deal negotiators are wrapping up the close. That way, he says, a core group of executives is pushing toward the goal while others catch their breath.

Executing an integration plan is always an arduous undertaking, admits Scott Werry. "We worry about making assumptions that synergies will be achieved sooner than reality tells us they will, because they always take time to execute." The other pitfalls, according to Werry, are the ramifications of today's condensed due diligence time frames. The major ramification, he notes, is the inclination to overestimate the potential of synergies, an overestimate usually based on a buyer's brief interchange with its target company counterparts. Avoiding that potential pitfall, he says, can depend upon the early inclusion of expertise in the target's industry to set reliable and realistic benchmarks based on past experience. From a seller investment banker's perspective, Brenen Hofstadter acknowledges a synergy realization process that can range from six to eighteen months, a wide range that can encompass numerous potential pitfalls. He recommends that bankers maintain a close relationship with the companies' existing management and the management that came with the transaction. "There is a strong correlation between the performance of the combined business short-term and the relationship between the parties," he says.

For Cathy Skala, synergy pitfalls can hide in the parameters to which the parties must adhere in the definitive agreement phase. The devil, she asserts, is often in the data. "Determine what data is sharable, maintain an orderly data room and obtain a clear understanding of the opportunities for synergy realization," she advises. The most significant pitfall, she says, is delaying the opportunity to gain synergies as soon as the deal is closed. The solution: Have plans in place to implement those synergies on the revenue and cost side. Those plans must be communicated to all parties, she counsels, especially plans regarding the implementation of cost synergies that may impact employees' jobs and lives. "The sooner the buyer can act on this, the sooner that management can definitively communicate with employees about plans and objectives and the timing of their implementation, the more successful the post-close will be in terms of synergy realization," Skala remarks.

Simon Gisby agrees. There is usually an overestimation of the synergies and an under-appreciation of the time and cost required to achieve a given synergy. As he says, "You have to give yourself truth serum when you ask yourself: Can I really do this in the designated time period?" To expedite the process on the acquirer side, Gisby recommends that buy-in from critical stakeholders possessing the experience and responsibility be obtained, and their participation agreed to as early as possible post-close in order to help ensure timely synergy realization. On the sell-side of the transaction, he adds, the risk of synergy identification is one of credibility, which leads, he says, to the issue of managing expectations, "because the seller desires to engage the buyer in discussion yet the buyer will only engage in discussion if the buyer is convinced that seller expectations are realistic." During the auction process, he has witnessed private equity firms asking, "Does the seller have realistic expectations of value, because if the seller's expectations are unrealistic, what is the point of expending the time and effort necessary for the buyer to get up to speed on the industry and the opportunity?" Gisby's advice to sellers is in the form of another question: "Are you sending a credible message to the buyer universe around value expectations?"

Declares Philip Torrence, "Successfully avoiding synergy-related pitfalls involves a diligence process that requires the participants to turn over the rocks and look under them. It is more than just a legal, accounting or business due diligence; it is synergy due diligence, which is a completely different animal, due to the soft factors."

Underestimating customer response to an acquisition, according to Andrew Lohmann, is one of those soft factors and is, in his opinion, one of the most dangerous synergy-related pitfalls: "It is easy to put on paper that a customer that buys from the acquirer and the target will react positively to an acquisition, but reality is not always on paper." A customer has a need to diversity its vendors. Simply combining a buyer and a target may not necessarily result in the anticipated dollar-for-dollar synergy. Lohmann advises conducting a customer channel analysis. Consider, he says, a case in which a platform company conducts its business through a distributor network. If that company is considering acquiring a target that maintains a different channel in which the target directly serves its customers, are synergies possible? "The target is now selling a product directly," Lohmann says, adding, "Does that hurt the feelings of the distributors the buyer has worked hard to please? I believe that there is much value to the financial and strategic buyers that have their fingers firmly on the pulse of the emotions and personalities that are inevitably involved in the typical middle market M&A transaction.

Conclusion

M&A strategy and the quest for synergy realization are married; tied inextricably to the success of any acquisition, from high-profile mergers to lower-profile, but equally intense, middle market acquisitions. History has proven, time and again, that any attempt to short-change either strategy formulation and implementation or the measured quest for post-close synergy realization will adversely impact the other and will add yet another company name to the growing list of deal casualties that continue, rightly, to spook and chasten M&A dealmakers worldwide.

TWO

The Art of New Beginnings

Cultivating The Deal From Origination to LOI

Part I. Finding and Pitching the Deal: the Beginning of the Beginning

A: Sourcing: The Start of the Mating Dance

Deal sourcing is the earliest step in the M&A mating dance that leads to the signing of a letter of intent, the first major milestone in the deal process. Sourcing is dependent on deal flow, which, in turn, is a product networking and research. There is no magic formula, no silver bullet for sourcing M&A deals, for juicing the deal flow process. Each deal begins as a result of months or years of assiduous care on the part of dealmakers, of lunches and contacts and information trading, of relationship building. Each dealmaker has his own way and style that suits their individual personalities, deal theses and corporate strategies. In short, there are as many deal-sourcing approaches as there are dealmakers. In the ensuing paragraphs, we will explore the origination approaches of four dealmakers, each representing a different professional sphere within the M&A practice.

B: The Investment Banker: 90 TMT Deals

"Instead of talking about other cable companies, I'm talking to every cable company owner." – Garrett Baker, President, Waller Capital Partners

Garrett Baker is an investment banker who is active primarily in the TMT (telecomm, media and technology) space since the 1990s, first with Bear Stearns and, since 1998, with Waller Capital Partners, where he is president. In 2014, he was named 40 Under 40 Dealmaker of the Year by the M&A Advisor. He is a sell-side banker, assisting private equity funds in the sale of portfolio companies in deals valued under $3 billion. Baker has personally been involved in at least 90 TMT M&A transactions during his career. His approach reflects that of his private equity clients; he remains close to PE portfolio companies during their five- to seven-year hold period, gauging a portfolio company's growth while devising an evolving go-to-market strategy, all the while staying in touch with every potential buyer in his subsector. "Instead of talking about other companies, he explains, "I'm talking to every cable owner," he says.

For its part, his firm stays connected to business owners in its wider TMT base, including metro fiber providers, digital media and e-commerce companies. "We do the same for entrepreneurs who start businesses," Baker declares. "We track them over time, because they tend to hold onto their companies longer." Baker and his firm also track divestures by large corporations. He and Waller maintain relationships with many big companies valued between $10 billion and $50 billion that are considered clients. "We're not expecting them to sell their companies, but they may need us for divestitures or to hire us on the buy side," he says. "Maintaining those relationships and making sure that we make our contacts aware of the deals we have done and the deals that are in our pipeline keeps us top-of-mind, which helps our cause when deals emerge that are in our wheelhouse."

Waller, Baker says, has never employed an internal business development professional. "The way we get most of our work," he declares, "is by doing our work." In his eyes, the most effective way to market Waller's capabilities to potential buyers "is for an owner of a company to see us selling another

> *"If we acquire a company that comes to our attention through an advisor or a banker, the board should fire me."* ~ *Villi Iltchev, Senior Vice President of Strategy and Corporate Development, Box*

owner's company, maybe selling that company to that owner, or showing it to that buyer and then selling it to another buyer for a higher price."

C: The Lawyer: Contributing Data to the Tech Ecosystem

"It's necessary to be an actual participant in your networks, beyond lunch dates." – Larry Chu, Partner, Goodwin Procter

Larry Chu, a Silicon Valley attorney, is a partner at law firm Goodwin Procter. It's the Silicon Valley style to foster networks, he notes, but not merely by taking potential clients to lunch. In Silicon Valley, he explains, "It's necessary to be an actual participant in your networks, beyond lunch dates." Chu cites Stanford futurist Paul Saffo, who coined the expression "contributor economy" to describe Google's business model. What Saffo means, says Chu, is that Google users are not simply consuming a service by using the Google search function. Instead, users are actually contributing their data to the Google ecosystem.

Chu says that being a participant in the tech community in Silicon Valley "is about fostering relationships with individuals on the buy side, showing them emerging companies and cool technologies that we are seeing in the marketplace, helping them deal source." Similarly, he adds, attorneys from his firm's sell-side practice introduce their contacts to potential investors, sources of human capital as well as to potential commercial relationships. "We try to participate in our community in a meaningful contributory way," Chu says. "We do this because we are blessed to be advisors in the technology space, where we are witness to so much dynamic activity in the form of emerging technology trends and new-born companies." Being a daily witness to such developments, he explains, "enables us to build robust and meaningful networks of people who turn to us for advice, to get a read on a new trend, or to unearth a potential deal." Assuming such a network building posture in the Silicon Valley mode creates top-of-mind awareness for dealmakers who can then expect a return on the information they have contributed to the tech ecosystem. His advice to dealmakers in and far beyond Silicon Valley: "A network that is nurtured and strong is the most effective way to source deal flow."

Chu's law firm also chooses not to employ business development practitioners to source deals. Instead, the firm relies on an internal marketing team. The marketing team, he explains, assists in arranging thought leadership events, "or fun things we can do with our friends and members of our client base, primarily private equity firms." In the tech world, he explains, business development professionals appear to lack the marketplace insight. "Having a big Rolodex doesn't work for us," he says, adding that, in a Silicon Valley environment, "business development professionals can neither talk intelligently about substantive topics that are relevant to our profession, nor can they participate in what is occurring in our marketplace." His perspective, he admits, differs from that of PE firms. "Private equity firms definitely need business development professionals to learn what is occurring in our world."

D: The Corporate Strategist: Adhering to Strategic Priorities, but Keeping an Open Mind

"If we acquire a company that comes to our attention through an advisor or a banker, the board should fire me." – Villi Iltchev, Senior Vice President of Strategy and Corporate Development, Box

Villi Iltchev came aboard at as Senior Vice President of Strategy and Corporate Development at Box, a Silicon Valley-based online file sharing and cloud content management service, after stints at Lifelock and Salesforce. His approach to sourcing, he says, begins with his company's corporate strategy. "I don't look to acquire companies that are not aligned with our three-year strategic objectives," Iltchev declares. He explains that he closely engages the Box organization and product teams to in order to garner a deep appreciation for their direction and, when possible, to influence that direction. When he achieves a solid understanding of corporate priorities, he adds, he is in a strong position to provide Box senior management with the appropriate relationships within every potential acquisition target.

Iltchev spends about 25 percent of his time communicating with external companies, some of which may become Box targets. He talks with two companies a day, ten companies a week, and five hundred companies a year. His corporate development team consists of two professionals and should, in combination with Iltchev's personal efforts, facilitate contact with about with about 1,000 companies annually. Says Iltchev, "This enables me to gain exposure to, or to have a relationship with, every company we may wish to acquire." In his relationship-building efforts, he explains, he communicates not only with potential immediate targets but also with emerging companies that might be worthwhile acquisition candidates years in the future. "I keep an open mind throughout this process," he says, "because part of my role is to find acquisition opportunities that may be off-strategy but are highly relevant and perhaps eye-opening and that might have an impact on our strategy."

His approach, then, is two-pronged: finding immediate acquisition targets and finding and tracking surprising and "exciting" new companies for possible future acquisition. This approach, he says, adheres to the template he established at Lifelock and Salesforce during the past six years. "This is where the world is going; the Internet is disintermediating the brokers of information and the brokers of relationships," he asserts. This trend, which started in the tech community, does not portend the end of the investment banking role in origination, Iltchev emphasizes. Instead, he says, it reflects the highly sophisticated nature of Silicon Valley deal sourcing, relationship building, and deal execution, "Because the velocity at which we in tech execute acquisitions is far greater than in any other industry."

For Iltchev, the rise of Internet speed-dating in M&A means that he has long since eschewed traditional M&A information sources. "I'm pitched every day, all day by individuals and companies selling access to M&A intelligence. I refuse to subscribe to any paid source of company information. I have no problem telling our board, 'If we acquire a company that comes to our attention through an advisor or a banker, then the board should fire me.' If the company brought to us from outside sources was an attractive company in an attractive market, I should not be finding out about it through an advisor."

To Iltchev, business development is relevant to platform sales, not to M&A dealmaking. As a strategic buyer, however, corporate development is his DNA. To him, as to most corporate development pros active in the dealmaking process, the primary mission of a corporate development team is to support corporate strategy through inorganic means. Yet in quadrants of the tech world, and at companies like Microsoft, for example, the corporate development team is the deal execution team. This team plays little if any role in strategy formulation, which, along with target selection, often emanates from individual business units. The corporate development function encompasses deal negotiation, process management and post-close target integration. However, in some tech companies, like Box, Salesforce and Lifelock, for instance, corporate development teams, in addition to deal execution, are closely engaged in strategy formulation at the product team level while also meeting annually with 3,000-4,000 potential acquisition targets. Iltchev, however, believes strongly that the corporate strategy should be owned, not by the corporate development team, but instead at the product level. "The individual who formulates strategy should be accountable for its implementation," he declares.

E: The Private Equity Executive: Ferreting Out Owners and Targets

"Ours is a very routinized sourcing process." – Bob Fitzsimmons, Managing Partner, High Road Capital Partners

A Citibank investm`ent banker before co-founding High Road Capital (a private equity firm focusing on small and middle-market companies) in 2007, Bob Fitzsimmons rejects the direct approach to deal sourcing. "We think that the direct approach, calling directly into companies to, try to engage senior management in a dialogue about selling their company, is a very low-probability proposition," He says. Instead, Fitzsimmons continues, High Road (which views itself as a generalist investor favoring manufacturing services, healthcare and media targets in the $10 million-$100 million range with a $2 million-$10 million EBITDA) prefers to ferret out companies with owners who wish to sell, and who have already engaged a banker or broker to help facilitate the sale.

Fitzsimmons' firm maintains a database of about 6,500 intermediaries, amounting to more than half the intermediaries in the US. High Road maintains regular contact with the intermediaries in its database via blast and specifically targeted emails, regular phone calls and visits to the cities where intermediaries are concentrated. The firm is also active in the Association for Corporate Growth (ACG), an unofficial M&A trade association, with attendance at ACG meetings or larger events. High Road covers its niche nationwide and in Canada through combinations of these methods.

"Ours is a very routinized process," says Fitzsimmons. "We rigorously track how frequently we are reaching out to every intermediary in our database."

High Road uses a customer relationship management (CRM) sales force to determine which intermediaries should be targeted for more frequent contact and those that require contact only once annually. Finally, special reports are produced aimed at aiding High Road in determining the number of intermediaries that have been successfully tracked.

Also routine for most private equity firms is the use of business development professionals to help source deals. In fact, Fitzsimmons recommends their use. "Our two business development professionals do nothing but source deals," he says. "In our business, transacting partners become busy doing deals and then fail to spend time prospecting for new deals." The result is that the transacting partners wait so long to ramp up prospecting following the close of a transaction that too much time is required to fill the deal pipeline. Says Fitzsimmons: "We have found that it is very useful to have professionals in the background who prospect fulltime because the sheer size of our prospect network of small middle market companies demands it." The head of the High Road business development team is a former investment banker who is adept at networking, a requisite skill in High Road's PE niche, Fitzsimmons explains: "We need an individual with strong networking skills, excellent presentation skills, who is very disciplined at making contact with thousands of individuals each year, is effective and efficient with follow-up, especially with contacts who have deals to discuss, is proficient and explaining our objectives to company owners and the reasons why they ought to sell to us."

F: The Asset-Based Lender: Focusing on Centers of Influence

"We source deals by leveraging our contacts and focusing on centers of influence in our origination approach." – Marc S. Price, Co-Founder, Executive Vice President, Loan Originations and Corporate Strategy, Salus Capital Partners

In M&A transactions, not all financing is derived from funding sources that are regarded as traditional. Some transactions, especially those when the buyer may require additional liquidity, are funded by asset-based lenders. Lenders such as Salus Capital, and the secured ending divisions of large commercial banks, provide acquisition loans collateralized by corporate assets, including plant, equipment, trademarks and accounts receivable, for example. This collateral is viewed as the primary source of loan repayment, while the borrower's creditworthiness is regarded as a secondary source of repayment. A defining characteristic of asset-based finance is an emphasis on monitoring the collateral, with the asset-based lender focusing on credit analysis and the value of accounts receivable and inventory in estimating the level of liquidity that can be made available to the borrower. A loan structure is then formulated. Collateral monitoring technology is deployed that is continuous and focused on the collateral, an approach that significantly reduces the risk of loss inherent in delayed intervention and/or asset recovery by the lender.

Marc S. Price, an M&A Advisor 2014 Professional of the Year finalist, is Co-Founder and EVP/Corporate Strategy and Acquisitions at Salus Capital Partners, the asset-based subsidiary of Harbinger Group, Inc., a diversified holding company. Price says that the Salus core management team averages 20-25 years of experience, with special and extensive expertise in asset-based lending to middle market borrowers. Says Price: "We source deals by leveraging our contacts and focusing on centers of influence in our origination approach." Such centers of influence can include private equity sponsors, loan workout professionals, commercial bankers, investment bankers, attorneys, former borrowers or a combination thereof.

Price points out that typical asset-based borrowers possess the following characteristics:

• Dependable and timely financial reporting
• Reliable systems and IT infrastructure
• A viable business plan
• Visibility to an exit or refinance
• A proven management team with relevant industry experience
• Portfolio diversification
• Familiarity with the asset class

Salus does not employ an army of business development professionals. Declares Price: "We'd rather spend the overhead dollars monitoring our portfolio." Nevertheless, he adds, his firm places corporate development professionals in strategic North American markets, such as Toronto, Atlanta, Los Angeles, New York and northern California. Their job: to make sure that the Salus brand and capabilities remain relevant and vibrant in each location.

Part II: Pitching the Client: What Works, What Doesn't – and Where

A: Establish Credibility

"Credibility is the major element of the pitch." – Garrett Baker, President, Waller Capital Partners

Credibility is hard earned. Once earned, it becomes the most essential ingredient in most client pitches, whether the dealmaker is a banker, a PE firm, a lawyer or a corporate. If even the slightest tear in the cloak of credibility becomes visible in the form of an errant fact or a wrong assertion, an opportunity valued at millions of dollars, tens of millions or more can dissipate faster than chimney smoke in a hurricane.

Waller Capital's Garrett Baker presides over an investment banking firm with hundreds of TMT deals to its credit, a big plus in any pitch. Credibility, Baker says, enables Waller to legitimately claim marketplace dominance: "We tell private equity firms that another investment bank may claim that it did X number of deals involving X dollars and that the firm is first in the league tables. Our response to such an assertion is that we do 60% of the deals in the TMT sector – and our knowledge of this business and this sector is deeper. Period." The major ingredients of his pitch: establishment of credibility, and possessing a thoughtful plan to sell the company. Baker says, "We don't hang out a 'for sale' sign and then summon buyers in the hope that they will show up." Instead, he explains to PE firms what he believes specific buyers are seeking and what his negotiating posture will be. He identifies the competitive hot buttons and explains, in detail, how he will push the right buyers to get the right price.

To asset-based lender Marc S. Price, credibility comes in the form of the ability to infuse clarity into complex concepts for the borrower's benefit: "You need to be relatable and concise in the pitch, and be able and willing to listen to what the client needs and then tailor a solution that fits a go-forward type of relationship in terms of addressing most of the potential borrower asks. Be certain, as a lender, that you will be able to live up to the pitch ingredients throughout the tenure of the relationship." Credibility is part of any first impression, and there is no re-do for a first impression, Price emphasizes.

B: A Concise Message Can Win the Day

"To me, the most essential ingredient of a successful pitch is a clear and concise message about what we can do for the client's business." – Bob Fitzsimmons, Co-Founder and Managing Partner, High Road Capital Partners

Private equity firms acquire companies, refine them, prime them for growth and sell them. It is not small task to convince a business to sell a company he or his family founded to a PE firm. That business owner, says Bob Fitzsimmons, wants to sure about the journey on which he and his employees may be about to embark: "To me, the most essential ingredient of a successful pitch is a clear and concise message about what we can do for the client's business." Fitzsimmons' PE firm, High Road Capital, specializes in buying smaller companies and then finding ways for those companies to grow. Most entrepreneurs are able to grow their companies' bottom lines to a certain point and then no more. Some owners simply do not wish to grow their company any further. Others wish to grow but lack the capital funding or the expertise to execute add-on acquisitions. In each of these scenarios owners are considering entrusting their company's fortunes to an external entity. That's when a firm like High Road enters the picture. At that point, Fitzsimmons says, his mission, in the form of a low-key informational pitch, is to explain to a business owner how Fitzsimmons and his firm operate." He tells them, he says, "that we pride ourselves on being fair, on being straight-shooters, that we are very focused on growing the companies that we acquire and have an excellent track record." These ingredients, he says, constitute a clear and compelling message that resonates with business owners.

C: Different Strokes for Different Folks in Silicon Valley

"Know what you're talking about; don't make a mistake." – Larry Chu, Partner, Goodwin Procter

Pitches are the same, but different, in Silicon Valley, because dealmaking there is the same, but different. For starters, says Larry Chu, consider the risk/reward thought process in tech deals. If he had to pick one element of how the assessment process differentiates tech M&A deals from all others, Chu picks this: In classic M&A, a target is selected for its inherent business attraction or technology value. Tech buyers, however, place an equal value on the cost of missing out on the opportunity to buy that company. That is a cost that is

"Make the best possible first impression." ~ Marc S. Price

difficult to quantify because it is unique to each buyer. In the blizzard of cloud deals during the past few years, gaining speed and scale in a vertical or sub-vertical technology has proven to be key. Declares Chu: "If you miss out on a target just because you're worried about the absence of classic support for the valuation, if you just look at it on a stand-alone basis, the deal assumes a different role in the risk-taking calculus, thus driving higher premiums than we are accustomed to."

Deal speed is another factor that differentiates tech deals from others. There are some big technology buyers that take their time but most buyers in the tech space move very quickly. A 30-day process is the new normal. In 2014, the time frame has been further constricted. One prominent acquisition, Chu points out, was done in less than 10 days: "These are big, complex deals done in very short time frames." Narrow windows are possible, he says, because tech companies are accustomed to moving fast in product generation and also pivoting quickly to seize opportunities.

A third differentiating factor, and one of the tech industry's major challenges, is access to tech talent, an extremely competitive endeavor in Silicon Valley. In deal pitches and in deals, there is a spotlight on how to best structure deal retention, which Chu calls "founder unfavorable." Issues crying out for resolution include persuading tech founders to revest portions of the deal consideration that they would otherwise receive, and have earned through several start-up years. "Now those founders are suddenly are seeing buyers ask for 20-40 percent and up to 80 percent of the deal consideration that they would have gotten to be revested over 2-4 years. You work hard and you think you are going to get that big payoff after you've been eating ramen for several years, but the payday is postponed or eliminated," Chu says. In many current tech deals, the carrot/stick approach is back in vogue. Revest is the stick. The carrots are go-forward incentive pools that are becoming bigger and more numerous. Chu comments: "These are human elements that need to be factored into the cost of a deal that are unique to the tech industry – and some of the numbers involved are staggering."

Although tech deal terms are somewhat more relaxed than in other deal spheres, they are more draconian in ways that are largely alien in other industries, especially around exposure to intellectual property (IP) issues. The reason for IP contentiousness: intellectual property is the major asset in most tech transactions. IP has become a litigious battleground, says Chu. "The patent regimes around the world differ country by country and are fraught with potential litigation-type issues. Even if it's not an issue that affects the functionality of product, it can attract real-dollar liability in litigation and mountainous legal costs." Companies, he says, have been burned in tracking damages around IP issues that exceed the typical 10-20 percent escrow. Now a second concentric circle has emerged consisting of IP-related hot-button issues, like privacy concerns and data security. "It's an ever-expanding circle of IP-related concerns," he remarks.

All of the above is a backdrop for tech dealmakers in making an effective client Silicon Valley pitch. Chu offers the following advice regarding the pitch's base expectation component at this turbulent tech moment in time: "Know what you are talking about; do not make a mistake." Being contextual, he points out, can be critical in outperforming in a pitch. "In dealmaking there is no such thing as one-size-fits-all." Recently, he says, his firm held a seminar for a large public company prospect that was seeking involvement in Silicon Valley dealmaking. The company is experienced in M&A dealmaking, but has traditionally used East Coast advisors and lacks tech dealmaking experience. During the seminar, Chu recalls, "We advised these participants that tech deal terms differ from others in rhythm and pace, in how the tech industry copes with human factors, such as retention. This is related to knowing your client and doing your homework. Including all of these factors in a pitch makes it more personal, in sharp contrast to a canned presentation." In this era, Chu concludes, clients and dealmakers do not lack for options. Therefore, he adds, "Liking the person you'll be working with becomes incredibly important; making a lasting personal connection very desirable."

D: Advice to CEOs from a Tech Pitch Catcher: Understand Your Product

"Good companies are not being sold, they are being bought." – Villi Iltchev, Senior Vice President, Box

For tech company CEOs looking to sell to a strategic buyer, Villi Iltchev of Box has this advice: the winning pitch starts with the product. Iltchev prefers to contact, or to be contacted by, CEOs of potential acquisition candidates, not by external advisors. "Good companies are not being sold, they are being bought," he emphasizes. Good companies, in Iltchev's estimation, possess three key ingredients: a well-informed CEO/founder able to succinctly and convincingly describe the product, a strong talent base, and, of course, the requisite business metrics.

"If a company comes to me through an advisor, it is, by definition, not a quality company," Iltchev alleges. A quality company, he says, is headed by a CEO/founder who is well versed in their company's products and customer relationships, and who is able to speak effectively about them. Unfortunately, he adds, some sellers either lack sufficient knowledge of their product or are unskilled presenters, which detracts from their ability to make a cogent and compelling pitch to a prospective buyer. Says Iltchev: "I expect the CEO to know his product and to be able to walk me through every decision made surrounding that product, to tell me how and why the product has been a winning formula for his customers and why his company's customers picked his product over a competitor's."

Iltchev also expects the seller to possess a deep pool of talent. As important as a company's product and technology may be, Iltchev says, absent a talented workforce, they are worth but a fraction of the company's true purchase value, even in a very large acquisition. He makes an effort, beginning early in the acquisition process, to build relationships with the target's talent. Iltchev emphasizes that those relationships "are incredibly important in building trust and must be authentic, genuine, honest, and transparent, even in the initial phases of the deal process." The reason: Without sufficient talent retention, there is no deal.

And the seller's business metrics must meet buyer expectations. Before he pulls the trigger on a deal, Iltchev says, he requires an affirmative response to his three questions: 1.) Does the product match his strategy; 2.) Is the seller team a team I can work with; 3.) Do the metrics measure up?

E: Advice to Asset-Based Lenders: Be Relatable, Be Accountable

"Make the best possible first impression." – Marc S. Price, Executive Vice President, Salus Capital

In weekly meetings with his staff, asset-based lender Marc S. Price makes it a point to simplify the essential ingredients of his firm's stump pitch to prospective borrowers. His checklist: 1.) Be relatable and concise in the pitch; 2.) Listen to the borrower's needs; 3.) Be able to tailor a solution that addresses most of the borrower's asks and facilitates a go-forward relationship; 4.) As a lender, be able to live up to the pitch ingredients throughout the tenure of the relationship; 5.) Make the best possible first impression. As the team leader, he says, "I hold myself accountable to the same standards as my team."

Part III: The Run-up to the Letter of Intent: the End of the Beginning

A: The Confidentiality Agreement: The Dancers Face the Music

"CAs are generally ignored." – Garrett Baker, President, Waller Capital Partners

"CAs are very significant." – Villi Iltchev, Senior Vice President, Box

Once the social phase of the pre-LOI dealmaker dance winds down, it's time to begin to get real, to tip-toe toward the potentially adversarial stage of the M&A dance that can begin with post-LOI due diligence and extend through the purchase agreement, the close and post-close integration. The formulating, negotiating and signing of the confidentiality agreement (CA), also known as a non-disclosure agreement (NDA), and then the Letter of Intent, marks the end of the beginning of the deal process.

The significance of the CA varies wildly among dealmakers. Some ignore it. Others obsess over it. At either extreme, however, the CA must be dealt with by the deal participants. What is significant about the CA/NDA is that it is the first formal agreement to be entered into in an M&A transaction. The CA, at its essence, is an arrangement wherein both parties in the transaction agree to share information with each other but to refrain from sharing that information with outsiders. The dealmakers also promise not to divulge the information that discussions between them are in fact occurring and are ongoing. In other words, the discussers are not allowed to talk about the discussions. Despite the disdain with which it is sometimes regarded, the CA/NDA is a serious legal document that mandates discretion by the dealmakers on both sides of the table.

According to Garrett Baker, buyers and sellers in the TMT space usually ignore the CA. "The CA gives the client some sense of protection that its information, and the news that it is involved in a deal, is not getting into the marketplace." But Baker also says that, in his opinion, the CA does not provide much of an advantage. "The players in the space know about a significant deal almost immediately," he remarks.

Attorney Larry Chu has a higher opinion of the CA's value. He views CAs as multifaceted agreements that address the disclosure and, more importantly, the use of confidential information, which is especially important in the tech world in which Chu is a practitioner. "When you are sharing trade secrets, business and details about your technology with a potential buyer," he says, "disclosure is damaging, but equally damaging is sharing the information and then not doing a deal, and the information you shared in good faith is put to uses which you did not anticipate or protect yourself from." Too often, Chu says, dealmakers fail to focus sufficiently on CA provisions that protect against such outcomes. CAs often contain a residual clause giving a buyer the legal right to use information gleaned from due diligence in building the buyer's own technology without paying royalties. "You could be giving up some very important use and ownership rights in a CA without any awareness of what you are ceding," Chu warns. Secondly, he cautions, care must be taken around provisions such as non-solicits, for instance, especially on the sell side. "In a competitive environment a seller is sharing environment details about employees. If the deal falls through, those employees can be picked off by competitors." Lastly, CAs set expectations and rules of the road around how and when information will be shared while defining the liability. "There are often provisions around not making representations on this information," Chu notes. There are rules about contacting customers and around sharing privileged information. "You have to be smart in a practical way in constructing a CA that includes the sharing of information about customers, because your M&A counterparty might be a competitor of some of those customers," he says. Chu's bottom line advice regarding CAs: Do not talk to a possible merger partner unless a CA is in place. "It's surprising how often that advice is not followed," he says.

Private equity exec Bob Fitzsimmons concedes that a CA is less important to him than to a strategic. But he also notes that, in a way, the CA is important to all dealmakers. "In order to know whether we want to buy a business, it is necessary for us to have information about the operation of that business. Therefore, the seller must be made to feel comfortable providing very confidential information to us." The most reliable way to provide that comfort, he says, is by having a well-drafted CA that will preclude a buyer from doing anything adverse with the information obtained.

Asset-based lender Marc S. Price takes CAs seriously. "We're an SEC-registered advisor and part of a public company. At the outset of every opportunity we produce standard NDAs and copies that are run in parallel with the origination effort but accountable to our general counsel." This procedure, he explains, allows all parties in a transaction to understand that his company is in receipt of privileged information and therefore obligated to live up to the terms of the CA.

Calling the CA "very significant," Villi Iltchev includes NDAs, but only later in the deal process when he wants to "get serious." The purpose of an NDA, in his opinion, is twofold: 1.) "I don't want to tell everyone in Silicon Valley that I'm having conversations with an entrepreneur, or that I've decided not to buy his company"; 2.) "I don't want the entrepreneur spreading the word that he is talking to me." However, under some circumstances, he says, the NDA can often prove to be mostly useless. "People from the company I'm talking to about a possible deal can say, 'I'm talking to a company whose name begins with B and ends with X.' " Old-school lawyers often request extra NDA provisions to guard against such eventualities, but usually fail to have their requests granted. One such provision, Iltchev says, is a residuals clause that states, in his words, "What you tell me that remains in my brain I get to keep and use as I see fit. I can destroy any documents you want me to destroy, but what you tell me stays with me." Never, he says, will he sign an NDA or even have a meeting with any individual who demands a residuals clause. Nor, he declares, will he, or has he ever, signed a non-solicitation clause. "We are in an Internet world now and I can find all the employees I want to find. Nor do

I want to send our HR department a list of companies that we can or cannot approach." Requests for these clauses occur frequently, he says. "I'm still asked for them. It's like a game, because the other party wants to see if they can slip this clause past me – but they can't."

B: Pre-LOI Management Meetings: How Often? How Useful Are They?

"We want to walk in smart – not only about the company, but also about the industry in which the company operates." – Bob Fitzsimmons, Co-Founder and Managing Partner, High Road Capital Partners

The jury is out on how many meetings buyers should have with seller management before the LOI phase begins. Bob Fitzsimmons prefers to meet with the entire senior management, not a single individual and not only the seller's owner. "When we have a first meeting with the seller, it is with the seller's management team. We like to show up well-prepared, having learned as much about the seller's business as possible. We want to walk in smart – not just about the company, but also about the industry in which the company operates." That means arriving with a set of questions that have been thoroughly thought through. The management responses to those questions, he says, will determine whether or not his PE firm proceeds with the acquisition. At his firm, Fitzsimmons emphasizes, pre-visit preparation helps them to "get up the curve faster, and to demonstrate interest and enthusiasm to the managers on the other side of the table."

Garrett Baker's investment banking role does not include conducting due diligence for counterparties. His key meeting is with his client, the seller. His aim is to determine how the client wants to present the business to prospective buyers and to make sure his Waller Capital team has a thorough understanding of the client's business. His major request of his client: "Make us aware of any information we need to know so that we provide you with the best advice on how to most effectively approach the market." His aim is not to glean every scrap of information about the client's operations. That is the buyer's role via due diligence, not his as the banker.

When he represents buyers, Larry Chu finds value in management meetings. He uses these meetings to scope out the deal terrain, especially when the transaction involves private company acquisitions in which there is no public market to set the benchmark for valuation, "when all you have to go on is data points." Pre-LOI, he explains, it is important to obtain the capitalization table to learn how much money has been raised and then meld that information with the expectations of venture capitalists. The objective is to triangulate on a value that makes sense to the buyer and also to the seller/founder and the investors. "I need the constituencies in the deal to be, if not happy, at least comfortable with the valuation," he says, "because it is too difficult to buy a company if the seller investors are not behind the sale." Especially in tech deals, he explains, it is important to get a feel for the management team, to learn if the team members are sharp, effective and prepared.

Management meetings are a sound way to determine the strategic fit of the seller into the buyer's organization. With a strategic buying binge underway in Silicon Valley, the buyer needs to know if the seller fits with the buyer's strategic roadmap. This is especially crucial in an industry in which traditional valuation methodologies are not those that need to be deployed in assessing a target. Pre-LOI, Chu explains, it is important for the tech buyer to acquire the needed information in order to put forth a proposal.

Tech strategist and corporate development ace Villi Iltchev insists that in a sizable transaction, "serious" buyers, after spending 2-3 days or less with a target's management team, ought to be able to garner the needed information as to whether they should acquire the business. "Our meetings with the target management at Box headquarters and at the target's company are also for relationship building purposes," Iltchev asserts. Then he spends a day, two at the most, with the seller team covering all major issues in a series of two-hour meetings, each meeting dedicated to a specific issue, usually sales and marketing, product, and vision. He also spends half a day with the target's engineers, "geeking out" on architecture and making sure, from a technology perspective, that the acquisition is the right fit. Often, he adds, there are follow-up conversation as his team proceeds with model building, valuation and creating a case for synergies. In aggregate, he concludes, three full days with the target management team is the maximum a buyer should expend in a tech transaction. It is at that point, Iltchev notes, that the target's founder should be advised that "a request for the buyer to spend more than three days with target management is a waste of the buyer's time."

For asset-based lender Marc S. Price, management meetings are an occasion to differentiate his team and company from other lenders in an M&A deal. "Our money is green, just like every lender's," he says, "but we have an unwritten rule at Salus that one of the partners must meet the individuals who run the company we are lending money to." More often than not, he says, "my gut will tell me whether or not the management team members will have the ability to navigate through their business plan." It's one thing, he says, to make a transaction underwriting decision based on a set of financials, audited statements, projections and other ancillary due diligence documents, "but there is nothing more telling than the perspective gleaned from sitting across a table from a potential borrower's CEO, CFO or other constituents." That is the best way, he emphasizes, "to get a clear reading on whether the borrower can uphold the rules, requirements and spirit of what is being contemplated on any credit facility that we close and fund."

D: Proceeding to LOI: To Go or Not to Go, What Are the Criteria?

"In tech, and certainly in the serious community of serial acquirers, you want to have greater than 90% certainty that at the end of due diligence, you will do this deal." – Villi Iltchev, Senior Vice President, Box

The response to the go/no-go dilemma is mainly the province of strategics and private equity firms – and lenders. Bob Fitzsimmons' PE firm, High Road Capital, maintains a rigorous decision-making process with regular check-ins from the High Road team before the firm submits a letter of intent. As is typical among private equity firms, at High Road the critical issues are discussed at Monday morning meetings. Every deal that has come into the house in the previous week is discussed. "We go around the table and solicit the opinions of all the investment professionals as to whether those companies are worth pursuing," explains Fitzsimmons. "If we get a strong positive consensus, we submit an indication of interest and arrange for our team to visit the company."

Following the visit, the team reports its findings to the firm's investment team. Based on those findings and the scope of the opportunity, the investment team will dig further into the opportunity, assessing its viability. If viability is likely, the investment team will conduct a financial analysis, run models and consult with lenders about deal financing and arrange for further meetings with the target's management team to discuss issues raised during the first meeting as well as obtain answers to questions that emerged from the financial analysis. Then the investment team decides whether to send an LOI. However, before the LOI can be submitted, the team writes a 20-30-page memo outlining the fundamentals of the target's business, the proposed outline of the financial structure, price terms, financing, an assessment of the investment risk and mitigants, the investment thesis, and an appraisal of the target management team, the company's position in the industry, and general industry trends. The completed memo results in a discussion by an investment committee at High Road's weekly meeting where a debate ensues about the merits of moving forward with the LOI.

For Villi Iltchev, the go/no-go decision hinges on a percentage. "In technology, and certainly in the community of serious serial acquirers, you want to have 90 percent or greater certainty that at the end of due diligence, you will do this deal," he says. A buyer's worst nightmare, he adds, is having to back out of a deal after a negotiated LOI: "As a buyer, you never want to be in that situation where you drag a seller through the mud, and then back out." The best way to avoid that eventuality, he says, is for the buyer to lay the groundwork first via relationship building, modeling, technology and strategic assessments and a briefing of the board of directors. Laying this groundwork, adds Iltchev, helps ensure that no matter what diligence reveals, absent a major negative surprise, the transaction will go forward and the buyer will not seek to renegotiate value.

For both Fitzsimmons and Iltchev, renegotiating terms and retrading price is an abhorrent practice. In tech, declares Iltchev, "I, as a buyer, am either going to do the deal or not. Diligence is not an opportunity to renegotiate terms." Iltchev says he has made 30 acquisitions in his Silicon Valley career and has backed out of only two during diligence, "One of those deals made it to diligence because of my poor executive leadership when I was unable to spend sufficient time with the target management team up front," He says, and in the second aborted transaction, he recalls, diligence-related issues were the cause. Bob Fitzsimmons' firm got its name, High Road, by pledging to always take the high road in negotiations with sellers, including a promise not to retrade price or to renegotiate terms.

As a lender in M&A deals, Marc S. Price, thanks to his firm's disciplined screening process, is able to provide borrowers a quick decision on funding. "We ask for essential information that helps determine whether the deal fits in terms of our business." As an asset-based lender, Salus Capital provides fully formulaic loans based on whether borrower assets securing the loan meet the Salus underwriting criteria. "Once we have the initial management meeting with the borrower, coupled with diligence, we can form an opinion, get to business terms and formulate an LOI," Price explains.

E: The Ebb and Flow of LOI Negotiations: Formalizing the Informal

"[The LOI] is less a proposal of marriage and more an agreement to go steady for the next 45 days." – Larry Chu, Partner, Goodwin Procter

For some dealmakers, its non-binding nature makes the LOI unnecessary. Once major items such as price and a grant of exclusivity are determined, they believe, it's probably more efficient to proceed to the definitive, and binding, purchase agreement rather than to become bogged down in the ebb and flow of more detailed LOI negotiations. At best, the LOI is a document that attempts to formalize the informal, to provide buyer and seller dealmakers with a framework for the ensuing phases of the deal execution process. While some have compared the LOI to a marriage proposal, others, like lawyer Larry Chu, balk at the comparison. The LOI, he remarks, is "less a proposal of marriage and more an agreement to go steady for the next 45 days."

Bob Fitzsimmons, however, prefers a detailed LOI. "We like to spell out as many of the transaction terms as possible at that point in the process." His preference, though, can result in LOI negotiations that are more complex. As for all dealmakers, price is the prime negotiating point on Fitzsimmons' LOI agenda. "We'll propose a price, but it's rare that a seller agrees immediately to our proposal." Ordinarily, he continues, "When we propose a price, we also have to determine how much pricing flexibility we have." Occasionally, he says, "We'll submit a price that is as high as we can possibly go." More often than not, though, he has a little more upward price flexibility beyond the price submitted in the LOI. The ebb and flow of negotiations, Fitzsimmons concedes, is part of every deal.

During LOI negotiations, buyer and seller attorneys are not yet facing off because the LOI is a preliminary document and non-binding. Typically, LOI negotiations focus more on the business aspects of the transaction and much less on the legal aspects of LOI provisions. Legal haggling is saved for the formulation of the binding purchase agreement. Nevertheless, explains Fitzsimmons, the LOI informally addresses the basic elements of the purchase agreement, including terms, warranties, baskets, survival period and caps: "We want to have those items laid out and agreed to in the LOI rather than leaving them for later, when they can create problems in the process. That's what we use the LOI for."

Larry Chu cautions that buyers and sellers need to maintain a balanced perspective during LOI negotiations: "The seller has to realize that the buyer cannot agree to everything." He also cautions that the LOI is not the definitive agreement. If the buyer is unable to commit to a point price or a point amount of escrow, the buyer should work within appropriate ranges. He advises the buy side to be reasonable as well, saying: "The buyer cannot announce that the only item he will commit to paper is a price or a price range." Instead, the buyer ought to understand that the seller has anxieties as well. The seller knows the buyer holds the purse strings, and thus the seller will strive to gauge degrees of deal and price certainties. Focusing on key items of concern at the LOI stage, Chu emphasizes, is a useful technique in arriving at a handshake deal, via the LOI, at an early stage of the deal process. To Chu, the most dangerous currents in the pre-LOI ebb and flow surround the buyer's desire to get a seller into exclusivity. The seller's awareness that granting exclusivity will result in sharply reduced negotiating leverage, with the buyer maximizing that point of leverage to extract as much detail and deal certainty as possible, is the major cause of tension in the pre-LOI stage, Chu says. As the buyer pushes to complete diligence, a commitment to the seller remains somewhat murky. The seller, meanwhile, pushes the buyer for additional clarity regarding price and deal certainty terms. The chances for a fouled deal atmosphere can rise. Not rushing through the LOI, whether buyer or seller, can result in a clearer deal environment and a lessening of tension.

For Villi Iltchev, the goals, strategies and motivations of buyers and sellers as they negotiate an LOI fall into several buckets. In tech deals, as in deals in other industries, price is paramount, because pricing discussions include the treatment of options, retention bonuses, holdbacks of equity and adjustments in working capital, for example. The areas of negotiation concern beyond pricing are usually the certainty of close and the duration of the exclusivity period, with the buyer ensuring the seller that diligence will focus on confirmation, not discovery. Iltchev refuses to become involved in talks about valuation, because, as he claims, "Both sides are looking to glean information from the conversation, and both sides will never agree on a methodology or a framework. It leads to a pointless conversation with no upside."

On buyer protection provisions, much of the debate centers on the size of the escrow and the duration of the general escrow. In tech deals, Iltchev says, exclusivity is fundamental and the only discussion focuses on whether the exclusivity period will be 30 or 60 days or somewhere in between.

There is much contention and negotiation around the definition of special reps and, of course, around how intellectual property risk is shared. According to Iltchev, lawyers enter the picture when discussions move to various indemnity provisions, which, in tech, involve frequently contentious talks about IP. IP negotiations can become so nasty, Iltchev says, that he is often tempted to punt on those negotiations until a week before the definitive agreement is signed and the deal closed, all of which is moot unless price discussions can settle around an acceptable ballpark figure. In Silicon Valley, buyers not only understand the seller's technology, they also understand that every tech start-up has institutional investors, which can present a level of complexity for buy side negotiators. As soon as buyers begin to negotiate a term sheet, Iltchev says, they are cognizant that the seller's founder has to negotiate not only with the buyer but also with the target's institutional investors. The good news, though, is that in most cases, the target's founder already favors the buyer. The buyer's mission, then, is to aid the founder in the founder's behind-the-scenes negotiations with the company's institutional investors. Fortunately, in the tech world, says Iltchev, M&A negotiators "know what they are doing and are experienced and competent." Terms are standard and public. According to Iltchev, outside of Silicon Valley, and especially on the East Coast, there is less standardization and more creativity.

For Marc S. Price, as an asset-based lender with a valuation background, a source of negotiation contention is the process of working through legal documentation regarding how the lender/borrower relationship is governed on an ongoing basis. "There should be a balance between business people and attorneys," he says. Business people should drive the process, not attorneys, he insists. In terms of valuation, in asset-based deals a non-binding summary of terms regarding the LOI is executed that is subject to diligence, which necessitates transparency and an upfront response by the secured lender regarding potential modification to loan structure or to LOI terms if diligence presents items that require modification. Any modifications, he advises, should be workable by both sides.

Conclusion

Every consummated M&A transaction marks not the end but a new beginning, a fresh start for a newly combined company whose presence will alter its marketplace. Getting to that new beginning, though, often requires the expert use of origination techniques and strategies, plus the determination to stay the course to the LOI and beyond, improvising when necessary and compromising tactically and skillfully to keep the deal process moving forward, cultivating the deal every step of the way, from the earliest stages to the signing of the purchase agreement.

THREE

Getting To Yes

From LOI to Closing The Deal

Part I: Due Diligence: Unlocking the Value

A. Diligence Begins Even Before the LOI

"The buyers that are playing to win are beginning their due diligence much sooner in the transaction process, sometimes even before the letter of intent is signed" – Ronald Miller, Managing Director, Cleary Gull

Due diligence is arguably the most important process in a deal and is fraught with opportunities and pitfalls. Buyers and sellers, advisors, attorneys, accountants and others (including bankers, insurance brokers and appraisers) spend days, weeks or months poring over financial documents, talking with customers and suppliers, evaluating management and labor agreements, appraising physical and intellectual property, and much more. The findings from the due diligence process impact virtually all aspects of the transaction and lead to the codification of a Purchase Agreement, which becomes the most important document in the consummation of the deal.

Intuitively it would seem that the longer the due diligence process, the greater likelihood the transaction will succeed – but recent research has actually found a reverse correlation – and interviews with experts for this chapter bear this out. Virtually all parties involved in M&A work – bankers, lawyers, advisors – agree that the due diligence process has become compressed, particularly during the past five years. Likewise, it should not be surprising that many advisors strongly recommend that due diligence commences even before the LOI.

Ronald Miller, managing director of Cleary Gull, an investment banking business in Milwaukee, WI, is co-head of a group of 16 who do about 15 deals a year involving industrial and consumer companies – "companies that make stuff and make money" – ranging from $10 to $200 million. About half of his deals are with corporate buyers and half with private equity funds. "We are really driving transaction timelines right now. If we can have a buyer close in 30 to 45 days instead of 75 to 90 days, that's a strong competitive advantage in today's marketplace," Miller says. "What that means is the buyers that are playing to win are beginning their due diligence much sooner in the transaction process, sometimes even before the letter of intent is signed." He adds that focused buyers are even hiring lawyers and accountants in advance of the final bid in order to differentiate their interest in the process. "This has been done in the larger deal market [$100 million-plus] for a longer time, but it's moving down into the middle market."

B. Compression Correlates to Increased Competition, Not Less Information

"We have learned that we can't–and we don't–staff our projects with juniors. Everyone on the engagement team is mid-level and up. Our clients cannot afford the time of having junior staffers participate in these compressed engagements." – Raymond Weisner, Senior Vice President and Managing Director, Valuation Research Corporation

James Dougherty, Partner in the Jones Day law firm of Cleveland, Ohio, has been involved with more than 100 transactions valued between $50 and $100 billion over the past 15 years. Dougherty says the pickup in private equity activity in the past 4-5 years is driving the compression of the Due Diligence process significantly. "Private equity sellers were starting to demand better terms – very low indemnity caps, limited protection from reps (representations) and warranties," Dougherty says. The quid pro quo has been private equity sellers recognizing that they need to satisfy the due diligence requests "up front," he says. How? Says Dougherty: "Basically, tell buyers, 'Look, we're not going to give you protection on the back end but in exchange we're actually going to give you real diligence on the front end and you'll have to get yourself comfortable with that mechanism.' It's actually gotten to the point now where there's not a ton of diligence and the process is fairly compressed and you're still stuck as a buyer with very limited recourse. It's a complete seller's market."

Dougherty also says "serial transactors" are in a much better position by doing multiple deals every year because – whether it's private equity or strategic – they become more efficient and streamlined during due diligence. "From what we've seen, if you're one of those out there who's ready to go and completely organized, you're going to find yourself at a pretty big advantage up front, both from a timing perspective and from being able to absorb the information that's there," he says.

A Dougherty side note: "That obviously puts more pressure on the diligence process generally – the more quickly you're doing things, the more chance for things to slip through the cracks or mistakes be made. So having an organized team where everybody knows the drill is a pretty important element to success in this environment."

Raymond Weisner is a senior vice president and managing director at Valuation Research, responsible for the development and quality execution of client engagements in all major industries. He was also the chief financial officer at two private companies. His team is engaged to help find a transaction's value, a process that has recently shifted. "It used to be that five to six weeks was the norm, now the norm is three to four weeks," Weisner says. "It's a big change. Five years ago we were quoting five weeks or six weeks. Now, we ask for four, and often are allotted less." To compensate, he says, "We have learned that we can't – and we don't – staff our projects with juniors. Everyone on the engagement team is mid-level and up. Our clients cannot afford the time of having junior staffers participate in these compressed engagements. That's our model."

Weisner says his flat organization model results in more efficient work flow and the required of his clients is less because his team has "learned to hone in on the critical issues and grasp them faster and zero in only on the required information and not cast a wider net regarding information requests or questions."

C. A Mountain of Relevant Data – Stored in a Cloud

"The VDRs make an auction process arguably more efficient because global buyers can be tapped without the need for them to expend significant resource in travel cost." – Steven H. Goldberg, Partner, BakerHostetler, LLP

Central to the trend toward more compressed due diligence timelines is technology. With the exponential, and cost-efficient, proliferation of cloud-computing and network storage over the past decade has evolved today's virtual data rooms. Whereas in decades past, relevant documents and data would be collected, stored and examined in a secure room at a law or accounting firm – a process that could take days or weeks – today's virtual data rooms can be set up in as little as two hours and securely accessed through a web browser from anywhere reached by the Internet.

Steven H. Goldberg is partner and national co-chair of the M&A practice at law firm BakerHostetler with more than 100 lawyers. He has been involved in the M&A business for more than a quarter of a century. He sees the emergence of virtual data rooms as one of the most significant developments in due diligence of his career. Says Goldberg: "The VDRs make an auction process arguably more efficient because global buyers can be tapped without the need for them to expend significant resource in travel cost. VDRs also make preparing for and conducting due diligence easier and more convenient, and relieve the target from confidentiality concerns over office visits by multiple parties."

While the virtual data rooms have produced clear benefits in terms of efficiency and cost, they also bring new risks to the due diligence process, Goldberg pointed out, by encouraging the justification of compressed deal timelines. This often results in the due diligence process being conducted concomitantly with the negotiation and drafting of the transaction documents. "So a buyer is often advancing down the path to signing before they have all of the pertinent data about the seller that they need," he says. "The danger in this

> "*Once you get to the LOI you should have at least 50 percent chance of closing.*" ~ *Dino Mauricio*

is that information discovered during due diligence may require a change in structure to the transaction, and it can be more difficult to effect that change once both parties are invested in an envisaged structure. While the tighter timelines may appear to point toward lower transactions costs, a necessary change in transaction structure often proves costly as well."

Dino Mauricio, Managing Director at KPMG Deal Advisory, has more than 25 years experience in dealmaking, advising in more than 75 transactions with more than $25 billion in combined market value. Because of compressed due diligence time frames – two to three weeks now, compared to two or three months in the past – Mauricio says, "data rooms have to be much more buyer-friendly, and that's why you have more virtual data rooms, much more emailing and intensive sharing of information. That wasn't possible in the past – the technology has certainly helped accelerate the pace at which information is shared between the seller and the buyer." At the same time, he says, there are real inconveniences and dangers for all parties: "Buyers still have the same requirements in terms of what they want to understand about the assets they are acquiring and how to effectively incorporate the risks and liabilities into the Purchase Agreement." Therefore, Mauricio says, buyers are doing more "pre-LOI confirmatory diligence" in order to focus on key issues and value-creation after the LOI – thus the strategic element of the acquisition must be confirmed in the target early in the process. This means more external advisors – lawyers, bankers, industry experts – have to become involved "to help that strategic buyer assess all the issues he needs to."

Private equity groups are better equipped to do rapid diligence from LOI to close, Mauricio adds, simply because "they're largely doing a financial transaction as opposed to trying to get consent from all their other divisions and customers, etc. This also implies that the success factors will benefit the larger funds that have very established processes for diligence…You often have multiple buyers and multiple PE firms. It's the ones who can go through the process more efficiently and they project themselves as being the more confident acquirers to the seller…they'll oftentimes get more attention and more responsiveness in a way that the other firms won't."

D. Is Deal Compression Really a New Phenomenon?

"If you go back to the era of 1990 through 2000 or 2001, I would say they make the pace of today's pace seem slow. There was an insane abbreviated pace for doing deals during the middle of that bubble period." – Robert Townsend, Partner, Morrison & Foerster

While 2014 was the biggest year for M&A in more than a decade, and deal time compression played a significant role in this, several longtime M&A advisors point out that there have been similar periods of compression in the past, most recently the so-called "dot-com bubble" of the late 1990s, and a similar period of big mergers in the 1980s. Indeed, time compression seems to correlate to the pace of activity in M&A in general.

Robert Townsend is co-chair of the Global M&A Practice Group at San Francisco-based law firm Morrison & Foerster. He has more than 30 years of experience in the fields of M&A, securities law, technology and intellectual property matters, leveraged buyouts, and venture capital, representing represented clients in more than 200 public and private company acquisitions, including numerous multi-billion dollar transactions. Townsend says: "As somebody who has been doing this for a long period of time, the time frame of deals does ebb and flow a little. If you go back to the era of 1990 through 2000 or 2001, I would say they make the pace of today's pace seem slow. There was an insane, abbreviated pace for doing deals during the middle of that bubble period. We see some uptick in pace today because we are back to an environment in which buyers feel they have to move with alacrity in order to compete for attractive targets. I would say less attractive companies, public or private, are proceeding at the same pace as always, but if you have a very attractive company, public or private, for sale, the sellers themselves will want to get it done quickly subject to whatever process maximizes the sales price, and the buyers will want to move quickly to preclude someone else from stepping in."

Townsend also sees the virtual data rooms enabling acceleration of the process, aiding both buyers and sellers in organizing the information that will be reviewed during due diligence. Particularly in directly negotiated deals, he counsels buyers to "get in early and try to persuade the sellers to use the buyer's standard form organization list for due diligence for information that would coincide with the due diligence request, because it's much easier for buyers to assimilate data and to get it into the hands of the right people internally to review if it is organized along the lines of how the buyer structured its own diligence process." He adds there is no industry standard form, but buyers will typically have their own internal form for a particular deal ahead of the seller, and the forms will differ from private to publicly held companies. Townsend adds that, because of Securities and Exchange Commission filing requirements, "There is already a great deal of information in the public domain when you're dealing with publicly held target companies." Private companies are a different story, he says: "You're starting from scratch... and so the request list is going to be much longer."

E. How Many Cooks in the Kitchen?

"Say one company is 60 percent of the deal, and one's 40 percent. But the people who are 40 percent don't think they're 40 percent – they think maybe we're better."
– Van Conway, CEO, Conway MacKenzie

From the seller's standpoint, Townsend says, "There is always a tension internally as to the number of what are called 'knowers' or people within the organization who are brought into the group of people who know this deal is happening. What people try very hard to do with an M&A deal is keep it as confidential as possible. If you have an accelerated process, from the sell side it means you may have to bring in more knowers earlier in the process before you reach a level of certainty that this transaction is going to happen than you might otherwise be comfortable with. It's very hard to make the necessary disclosures without having the people you know are responsible those areas participating in the process and providing that information." He notes that all of these "knowers" also have "day jobs," and may see the additional demands on their time put on by compressed due diligence process as an inconvenience.

Benjamin Perkins is a Senior Managing Director and the US Life Sciences Sector Leader for Ernst & Young Capital Advisors, LLC, with 17 years of investment banking and corporate finance experience and $7 billion worth of closed deals. Because of deal time compression, Perkins says, his team now generally takes 1-2 days internally prior to submitting the LOI "to understand exactly what are we going to focus on as part of the diligence process. What are the 5-10 key issues that we need to get a better understanding of to get a better value? Are we going to do it aggressively or are we going to slow burn? Historically what we would do as an M&A advisor would be to pick over the data that we believed to be of value and then come back and have a boardroom discussion of – okay, here are the things that we found, here are the things that we're concerned about. In today's environment, you really need to go into that LOI period with 'Here are the top 10 things I need to understand.' It may be a financial question, it may be a reimbursement question, it may be a question of geographic footprint, but there are a number of issues that you as management, you as an advisor, that you want to feel darned sure about before you sign anything in a Purchase Agreement."

Van Conway is a founder and CEO of Conway MacKenzie, a middle-market M&A advisor firm with more than 40 years in the business. Over the years he's seen "bad deals that shouldn't have been done" and maintains that "due diligence that is rushed puts all the risk on the buyer. We're not in that stage yet but we're moving in that direction." Among all the value considerations examined during the due diligence process, he notes that personalities can often influence the outcome more than data. "You get into deals where, say, two CEOs are going to merge. Who's going to be the new CEO? Well, trust me, the guy not getting the job might tank it. It happens in corporate America. We call it a 'dating issue.' Why spend a money analyzing each other if one guy doesn't get it, he'll tank the deal."

Likewise, Conway observes, the more people involved in the deal, the greater the risk of internal opposition. "Say one company is 60 percent of the deal, and one's 40 percent. But the people who are 40 percent don't think they're 40 percent – they think maybe we're better. Then they find out 'we gotta move,' 'my boss is getting swept out.' The personal side of the personnel issues, including the headquarters, can blow deals up. So we say, you're got to have these issues negotiated before you spend hundreds of thousands of dollars in Due Diligence and then find out at the altar, we never were going to get it done."

"A deal is three things: How much money you get, when you get it, and why you might have to give it back." ~ Ronald Miller

Part II: The Purchase Agreement – the Formal, Enforceable Legal Document

A. The Emergence of Rep and Warranty Insurance Alongside the Purchase Agreement

"Basically the way it works is pretty similar to your car insurance – you've got an overall cap, you've got a deductible and you've got a premium." –
James Dougherty, Partner, Jones Day

Colorful as always, Conway likens the signing of the Purchase Agreement to "finding out if your wife likes you before you marry her. It's like a pre-nup agreement. If something goes wrong, you go to the agreement. Paragraph 64. Yes, that's what it says." The Purchase Agreement, all agree, is the document you have to live by in a merger or acquisition. "The quality of the Due Diligence will result in the quality of the Purchase Agreement," Conway says.

"The Purchase Agreement is the deal; its significance cannot be understated," says Steven Goldberg of BakerHostetler. "The Purchase Agreement is the final and only memorialization of the entire business agreement between a buyer and a seller. It is the document that will govern how the business is run between signing and closing and then what recourse can be had by the purchaser post close if aspects of the business were misrepresented or unforeseen litigation occurs. Most Delaware courts are now realizing that words have meaning and are more loathe to go outside the four corners of the agreement if interpretation inside the agreement is possible." Also important: Purchase Agreements can be significant as a precedent for subsequent transactions. "Parties will often stick to, or conversely be held to, certain positions taken in a previous Purchase Agreement," Goldberg said.

While important, James Dougherty of the Jones Day law firm in Cleveland, says the Purchase Agreement's "role has diminished substantially" during the current cycle of M&A. One reason – "you have a very limited amount of recourse as a buyer in most deals these days. You're going to get a relatively skinny set of reps and warranties, and your remedy for breach of rep is going to be the indemnity, which is going to be fairly low." In a lot of deals middle market deals today, Dougherty says, the indemnity caps range from 3 to 10 percent of the purchase price.

The other reason why the Purchase Agreement has become less important, he says, is "the emergence of Rep and Warranty insurance." A relatively new phenomenon in M&A, rep and warranty insurance. Rep and Warranty policies insure buyers and sellers against the risk of inaccuracy, falsity or a breach of the representations and warranties contained in a Purchase Agreement. "Basically the way it works is pretty similar to your car insurance – you've got an overall cap, you've got a deductible and you've got a premium," Dougherty says. "So the private equity seller really started this. They basically said: 'we're not going to wind up giving you indemnities. When we sell a business we want to distribute cash to our partners and we'll give you a low cap for maybe one year.' And buyers were in a conundrum because they wanted these businesses but they weren't comfortable with the low (indemnity) cap. Rep and Warranty insurance has emerged as a way to fill that gap."

DEAL NOTES

Rep and Warranty Insurance from the Broker Perspective

Jay Morascak is Senior Vice President at Aon Risk Solutions in Cleveland, and previously was with the M&A group at Wells Fargo Insurance Services. He has worked with James Dougherty of the Jones Day law firm on a number of transactions that have been insured by a Rep and Warranty policy. "Rep and Warranty insurance has been around for a while but it's really been gaining a lot of traction in the last 18-24 months. Even 36 months ago, people were just starting to look at it. The marketplace was becoming more receptive to it so the underwriters were getting more sophisticated in doing it because deals were sometimes not happening or were running into significant hurdles. So the insurance industry looked at that as an opportunity to try to put a product in place that will potentially help both buyer and seller to reduce the uncertainty and also help with a cheaper way of getting the deal done."

Of course, just as in writing a Purchase Agreement, writing a Rep and Warranty policy involves diligence and the devil is in the details. "Every situation is a unique set of challenges, so what we've seen is a growing sophistication within the insurance marketplace, and also with buyers and sellers, of using Rep and Warranty products as a way to help facilitate deals," Morascak said. "And underwriters have become much more sophisticated in terms of the M&A world. We have former M&A tax people, former M&A lawyers who are now in the underwriting side of it."

As underwriters have become more sophisticated as assessing M&A risk, insurers have become more willing to write policies. But because each M&A deal is so unique, insurers and underwriters are limited in using "boilerplate" language in their Rep and Warranty policies, Morascak says. "We would consider this an untraditional insurance product and each transaction is underwritten specifically given the situation and crafted to the deal."

Rep and Warranty policies have had more use in larger deals, Morascak says, but are becoming more common in deals under $100 million. "Not every deal uses Rep and Warranty insurance but I would say it's becoming more looked at – it's a standard checklist item in most deals today."

B. Purchase Agreement Is Drafted Concurrent with the Due Diligence Process

"There's always been a balancing act... particularly after the LOI of when you start documentation and when you complete diligence." – Dino Mauricio, Managing Director, KPMG Deal Advisory

The due diligence process has always paralleled the drafting of the Purchase Agreement, and it has always been a balancing act, says Dino Mauricio of KPMG. "In the past you'd want to complete as much of the diligence as you could before you start with the documentation. Why? Because as you go forward in the diligence the chances of actually completing the deal go up. But then once you start documentation it really takes away time and resources away from what otherwise could be used for diligence. So there's always been a balancing act...particularly after the LOI of when you start documentation and when you complete diligence. What's happened with the compressed time frames, you automatically do both. Because once you get to the LOI, you've got an exclusivity period and you're much more confident that you can get a deal done."

Issues can arise during the parallel track of due diligence and drafting the Purchase Agreement. Unexpected discoveries or surprises that are brought to light during due diligence can be very distracting and result in major changes in the documentation. "Sometimes you have to bring in different types of lawyers, or there's an outside party that has to advice on that. It adds another layer of negotiations," Mauricio says, adding that cultural issues and cross-border issues can also complicate the parallel processes, he says: "Technology companies being acquired by brick-and-mortar companies – you have these cultural factors that can enter into the negotiation process that are still being ironed out during the due diligence." Additionally, buyers often introduce financing considerations during the twin-tracked due diligence/Purchase Agreement processes. "Buyers have do so some contracting with financiers and that just increases the amount of that's being done in the final stages of this period before close." Mauricio said.

Steven Goldberg of BakerHostetler offers some practical advice for dealing with these kinds of inevitable issues: "We believe that the best way to deal with these type of conflicts is not to take them personally, and to maintain a cooperative, forward-thinking approach to getting the transaction done as efficiently as possible in a manner that most closely resembles the originally agreed deal. This often requires frank, no-nonsense discussions between the parties representatives (often the lawyers) so that some of the emotion may be taken out of the equation and the parties can focus on the end goal."

C. Overcoming the Obstacles to Doing a Deal

"When the process is not organized is often when mistakes or unnecessary misunderstandings occur." – Steven Goldberg, Partner, BakerHostetler

"Diligence is a fairly adversarial period. In almost every transaction my team gets frustrated with the buyer and questions whether they'll be a good partner for the management going forward," says Ron Miller of investment bank Cleary Gull. "The advice I give buyers in every transaction is: Ten days into the deal, just go have a beer with the management team. Don't have your daggers out. Don't discuss questions and challenges in diligence, just build a relationship, because these are the people you're going to be backing to drive your value creation going forward."

Miller adds that "A deal is three things. How much money you get, when you get it, and why you might have to give it back."

Ben Perkins of Ernst & Young says most of his time during the lead up to Purchase Agreement period is spent on indemnification issues. Because of the compressed time frame, parties don't feel like they've had the time to address some issues the way they would have liked with more time. "We're also spending a lot of time negotiating earn-out payments and milestone payments and things like that where, if there is a discrepancy about what the value of the acquisition may be, you try to capture that through ongoing payments if certain milestones are met," Perkins states.

Organization among the parties and working through the process together is often the most important method for refining the purchase agreement, says Steven Goldberg of BakerHostetler. He adds: "Knowing when, and in what form, to expect comments or revisions from the opposing party is critical so that ample time is provided for to give the purchase agreement a "clean read" and to receive the required business thoughts and specialists [i.e., tax, environmental, employment] input. When the process is not organized is often when mistakes or unnecessary misunderstandings occur."

Robert Townsend of law firm Morrison & Foerster says one of the critical time elements and most important aspects of diligence is reviewing the financial statements of the target company. They are released periodically and are historical-looking, but also contain projections for future periods: "...Both of those are critical sources of information on the performance of the business that you're buying. The projections are usually delivered very early on and don't change much during the deal." He also notes that deal teams have to be careful not to announce or sign a deal just before new earnings are being released or financial information is being updated: "You as the buyer are going to want to have those financial statements in hand before you sign the bottom line." If new financial statements during the process reveal fundamental changes in the performance of the business, Townsend says that discovery "can have ramifications for whether the deal goes forward and, if so, at what price."

Another important issue is disclosure of sensitive agreements, Townsend adds, particularly because many deals involve competing companies. Prices and other terms in those agreements are sensitive and cannot be shared for obviously competitive reasons as well as anti-trust concerns, he says: "You need to stage the timing and the manner of disclosure of those so that as the seller you are not tipping your hand too much to the buyer and so that you manage legal risk around anti-trust and other things." Likewise, licensing agreements for products or intellectual property must be carefully scrutinized in diligence and have often become dealbreakers if issues are not resolved, particularly in the high-tech sector.

D. Getting to the Signing of the Purchase Agreement

"In general once you get to the LOI you should have at least a 50 percent chance of closing… If you have a good LOI, you have a 75-80 percent chance of closing."– Dino Mauricio, Managing Director, KPMG Deal Advisory

The signing of the Purchase Agreement usually signals the passing of the deal baton from the investment banker who negotiated the deal to a lawyer who finalizes the details. Either party can draft the Purchase Agreement, but in most cases the buyer drafts the document, often long before the LOI.

"Ideally, if you're a buyer in a perfect world, you would do all of your diligence first, and then you would turn to doing the contract, because you're doing the contract with the most information possible. But that rarely happens," says attorney M&A attorney Robert Townsend. "So from a buyer's standpoint, assuming you are moving in parallel, one of the most important things is to insure that the definitive agreement does not get too far in front of the stage of due diligence so that you still have the ability to go back and modify the contract to reflect things that have come up in diligence, and that the seller cannot accurately say you have passed on doing so because you have already resolved those points. From the seller's standpoint, there is always the balancing act of insuring that you have disclosed at an early stage the material information that could impact the principal terms of the transaction to minimize the risk that you are re-traded later by the buyer," states Townsend, further adding:

"Sellers typically have less and less leverage as the deal goes on."

Dino Mauricio of KPMG points out: "In general once you get to the LOI you should have at least 50 percent chance of closing. In general, issues that can break deal are material discoveries or unexpected issues. If you have a good LOI, you have 75-80 percent chance of closing." He says after the LOI stage it's important to have a "firm timetable to close" and that the people involved in the process are the decision makers. "You don't want to have people there that have to go check back with other people – it just complicates things. And make sure you line up all the relevant advisors and industry experts that are needed."

Leading up to the signing of the Purchase Agreement, the intermediaries should be playing big roles, Mauricio says: "One of the reasons you hire lawyers and bankers and consultants is they have prior transaction experience [and] familiarity with issues in that industry or with this deal, so they can quickly get to the right terminology in the Purchase Agreement. If it's just a buyer and seller trying to hash out terms, it really takes away from the process. The lawyers and transaction advisors really insure that what is required gets captured in the purchase document. Again, the decision makers have to be involved so that as you're working through the issues and there's accountability for deciding what's involved in the documentation."

Particular value that an investment banker may add, Ronald Miller says, is dealmaking history: "I've shown 35 transactions to [one PE firm]. We keep a database. We actually know their contract terms on what the buyers are willing to do. We know their negotiating styles. We track buyer behavior. We share. Again, this industry has gotten a lot more sophisticated – when we are presenting buyers and proposals to our sellers, we talk to our sellers about the buyers prior behavior, whether they close on their Letter of Intent, how much money they have, how they have negotiated in prior transactions. We capture their behavior and that's incredibly important to the ultimate choice of who their partner should be. We reference check almost every transaction. I'm in the Midwest. We actually care who we sell to."

"There also has to be a commitment to 'deal point resolve,'" Mauricio adds. "So any deal point that has been resolved has to be untouchable. You can't have a situation where you're resolving a third thing and the buyer goes back and tries to rehash a prior point. That's a ground rule that's been place for awhile – otherwise everything gets to be interdependent and you never come to an agreement."

Finally, "you have to know when the negotiations aren't being productive," Mauricio says. "Even some of the best strategic acquirers will get involved in negotiations where because of their prior success they feel like they can make the deal happen by brute force, or by throwing enough lawyers in there or pounding the table. But at some point, if the Purchase Agreement can't come to a common understanding, it's best to just break those negotiations off because you'll just waste time and resources that could otherwise be spent on another deal."

Part III. The Close: the Beginning of the End

A. The Advantages of Simultaneous Closings

"It mitigates one of the major risks in M&A which is the deterioration of the business once an agreement has been signed to sell the business." –
Robert Townsend, Partner, Morrison & Foerster

In today's M&A marketplace, parties sign the transaction documents and close on the deal simultaneously whenever possible, the best dealmakers say, although deferred closings are sometimes inevitable, particularly where shareholder approval, regulatory consent or other matters are involved. A simultaneous signing and closing benefits both parties because it eliminates transaction risks – such as a natural disaster or loss of key customers – during the intervening period. A simultaneous closing can save time and eliminate the need for lengthy negotiations over who should bear the risk of such events.

"Simultaneous signings and closings are advantageous for both parties because they are often less complex, less time-consuming and less costly," noted BakerHostetler's Steven Goldberg. "They also provide certainty in the sense that a signed deal is, in fact, closed. That's not always doable because of regulatory requirements like obtaining Hart-Scott-Rodino {a federally-mandated pre-merger requirement} clearance or a permit upon a change of control."

Says KPMG's Dino Mauricio: "Simultaneous signing and closing is the default. You would love to have both parties sign and close at the same time and that eliminates transaction risks during that intervening period. It means you don't have to raise any uncertainties on what could happen between signing and closing such as something happening with the business or the customer or a supplier. It could be some environmental item or some disaster. So it really saves time and resources."

Morrison & Forerster's Rob Townsend says of a simultaneous closing: "It mitigates one of the major risks in M&A which is the deterioration of the business once an agreement has been signed to sell the business. It's just human nature to have people who are running the business – the sellers – pay less attention to the business once a buyer's committed to buying it and before a subsequent closing can happen. That is not good for the buyer or the seller. It's not good for the buyer because the business that you're buying is not necessarily being well run while you're waiting to get to closing, and it's not good for the seller because their management team and their people are distracted and may be looking for other jobs and they may in fact find themselves not closing the deal at the end of the day – in which case they will be taking back a business that has been ignored for a period of time.

DEAL NOTES

M&A Advice from the Corporate Perspective: Downing Wellhead Equipment

In 2014, the M&A Advisor's Energy Deal of the Year (up to $100 million) was the acquisition of Downing Wellhead Equipment by Argonaut Private Equity.

Gene Downing, who founded his company in 1980, ran a complete wellhead company providing manufacturing, remanufacturing and field service to the oil and gas industry. He had expanded the business over the years and many of his original employees were still with him 35 years later.

"The reason I sold it: I'm an old fart," Downing says. "I used to think, 'I'm never gonna die,' that I would just keep on doing what I'm doing. And then I was driving down the road and Hank Williams, Sr., came on [the radio]....his song, 'I'll Never Get Out of this World Alive.' "

Downing started looking around 3-4 years prior to selling his 80 percent of his company in April 2014 to Argonaut Private Equity. He brought in a group who he says did a terrible job – "they were dumber than a box of rocks"– valuing his company. Meanwhile, word got out of his interest in selling and he was inundated with interest. "They were sending flowers and I was getting phone calls; everybody was coming out of the woodwork."

Something about a flyer that came in the mail from Allegiance Capital, a Dallas-based investment banking firm, caught Downing's attention.

"There was something about [the investment bank} that seemed to me that these folks were different. Maybe it was a God thing," he says. "So my wife and I jumped in a plane, went down to Dallas, went to their office and talked to them, looked at them. And I was impressed with their demeanor. I was impressed with their sincerity. And then I walked up and down their hallways, and saw all the tombstones [ads] on the deals they'd done and I recognized some of them….and man, I was impressed. They did some serious work here.

"Then when they started doing the work, I was extremely busy – working 50-60 hours to keep things going because we were in the middle of a big boom – and they really added so much value. When I first started it was like drinking from the fire hydrant – so much information. They walked me through everything. I've never seen anything that professional. They were on the same wavelength as we were. They understood the business. And that's what really makes the difference."

The process took about 6 months – the number of companies interested exceeded 50 and were winnowed down to about a dozen before Argonaut made an aggressive move to make the deal. "We had previous dealings with them – they were known to us and it was a good working relationship," Downing says of Argonaut. "Both parties knew what the others were looking for.

"My original employees were very, very important. I've got some of my original employees who have been here 35 years. I spent a couple of years thinking about this – looking at it and analyzing it to insure that the person I sold it to would have the same values I did."

Allegiance Capital managed the complete marketing and sales process for Downing Wellhead. This included: preliminary valuation, marketing the company both domestically and internationally, soliciting Letters of Intent and negotiating them, managing due diligence with buyer, structuring, financing, and executing the closing.

"It was a privilege to work with Gene and Jo Downing during the sale of their company," said John Sloan, Vice Chairman and Senior Managing Director of Allegiance Capital. "Their professional approach to the process and their dedication to working with us and with potential buyers to overcome any issues that developed, enabled us to successfully craft a transaction that worked well for both the buyer and seller."

B. Why Deferred Closings?

"The buyer wants control of the business and the seller hasn't sold the company so they want freedom in running their business while they still own it." – Ronald Miller, Managing Director and member of the firm's Board of Directors, Cleary Gull

Beyond regulatory hurdles, that can take months or years and are a fact of life in many industries, there are advantages to having deferred closings. BakerHostetler's Steven Goldberg points: "Simultaneous signings and closing are less common in asset transactions in which there are a large number of consents that need to be obtained, or complex share transactions where new entities need to be created and assets transferred amongst subsidiaries and any transaction in which regulatory approval is required. The obvious drawback of separate signings and closings is the lack of certainty that the deal will close. The format is often a 4-8 week lag time between signing and closing during which the parties can get the required regulatory approvals or do the necessary housekeeping to effectively transfer the assets at closing."

Investment banker Ron Miller says: "The benefit of a delayed closing is you want to get your customer calls and final approvals after you know you have a deal. So it would be nice only to call customers after you have a signed agreement and the buyer can be conditioned to close the transaction to his satisfaction with customer interviews – they need a reason to change the price or back away from the transaction." But, he adds, sellers typically resist many conditions that buyers seek between signing the Purchase Agreement and closing the deal, which is usually a few days to a month. "The buyer wants control of the business and the seller hasn't sold the company so they want freedom in running their business while they still own it. So it is very difficult to agree on a mutual set of conditions between signing and closing." Miller said 80-90 percent of Cleary Gull's transactions are simultaneous sign-and-close deals.

A simultaneous closing may also increase shareholder risk since a target may have to go public about the transaction by soliciting shareholder consent and contractual consent from customers or vendors or other third parties minus a binding contract in place. In these situations, a deferred closing structure enables both parties to determine the rights and remedies of each party in the event the required consents are not obtained.

"Private equity firms are happy either way, but with a deferred closing they can have more leverage by discovering {more about the target}, but at the risk of not doing the deal," noted Dino Mauricio of KPMG.

C. Closings: Almost, Not Quite, at the Finish Line

"There should be a close proximity between the definitive agreement and the wire transfer. If something happens then, you've probably got a bigger problem than you think," – Van Conway, CEO, Conway MacKenzie

Typical closing deliveries include the following:

- The operative transaction document, such as the Purchase Agreement or the merger agreement, if not already executed.

- Board and stockholder consents authorizing the transaction.

- The corporate secretary's certificate certifying the accuracy and effectiveness of the relevant authorizing resolutions and charter documents of the target company.

- Legal opinions.

- Ancillary agreements and documents, such as promissory notes, bills of sale, employment agreements and escrow agreements.

- Consideration (e.g., stock or cash).

- Financing agreements.

- Regulatory approvals.

- Evidence of third-party consents.

- Evidence of the release of any liens.

"The big category is post-closing obligations," says Dino Mauricio of KPMG. "That includes all the representations and warranties, non-compete agreements, non-solicit or non-hiring requirements, certain indemnifications. Those should all be in place at the closing and survive after the closing."

He adds that by the LOI stage, the parties should already have a list of deliverables needed at closing to avoid later misunderstandings. A consensus among the Best Dealmakers interviewed is that there are very few closing day glitches today due to the intense diligence process.

Robert Townsend of law firm Morrison & Foerster maintains that the important deliverable is the "purchase price – stock or cash." Investment banker Van Conway says: "There should be a close proximity between the definitive agreement and the wire transfer. If something happens then, you've probably got a bigger problem than you think. It might be buyer's remorse. Psychological things can happen. Or sellers can get anxious."

Steven Goldberg of BakerHostetler points out: "Consents and regulatory approvals are often the areas where issues arise, as those items rely on third parties outside the immediate scope of the transaction. These hiccups can be remedied by proper planning ahead of time, but may also require both the buyer and seller working cooperatively to put pressure on the third party to accommodate the transaction timeline. An appropriate board record is also important to ensure that management is apprising the Board and for the Board to ultimately evidence to shareholders if necessary."

Goldberg notes that a new development in 2014 has been an increase in activist involvement in M&A. "Activists are one engine driving the process for splits and divestitures," he says. "The motivation behind activist activity is the belief that certain splits or divestitures will unlock value because the market will value the pieces individually higher than it would the company on an aggregate basis."

D. In-Person Versus Virtual Closings

"Anyone can do a deal, but to have success and some confidence in the marketplace, that requires some work." – Dino Mauricio, Managing Director, KPMG Deal Advisory

Historically, closings occurred in person with representatives of both parties and their counsel present. It is now common practice, however, to complete closings by phone, fax, e-mail, and/or wire transfer without an in-person meeting. The advantages of a virtual closing are obvious in global deals, getting the signees around a virtual table much more easily than an in-person closing. Virtual closing didn't exist 20 years ago and were a novelty even a decade back. Now, virtually everyone interviewed for this edition of Best Practices of the Best Dealmakers says they are the predominant form of closing.

"There's hardly ever an in-person closing," said investment banker Ronald Miller of Milwaukee. "I can't remember when I've been to one. It's very important that all stakeholders are available on the day of closing and 24 hours prior to closing. There tend to be a couple of key phone calls. I haven't had games played during closing – those usually happen more like a week of two before. There's more nail-biting then. My job in closing is to defend the price and the process."

Nonetheless, in-person closings still occur, and some transactions, including those involving the sale of real estate, require that certain documents be signed in person.

Dino Mauricio of KPMG is one who sees merit in the in-person process: "I've seen successful deals handled either way, and in my mind the deal is going to happen or not whether it's in person or a virtual closing. It does not impact whether the deal gets done...Once you get to that point, it's really a convenience factor and also how the parties want to consummate their transaction. It shouldn't impact the success of the deal. That said, there are some advantages and disadvantages either way. One is the handshake and trust factor. There's certain things you can read into the other side when you do an in-person closing."

Mauricio, is also involved in after-closing issues and consulting with newly merged or acquired companies. "Anyone can do a deal, but to have success and some confidence in the marketplace, that requires some work. And I think an in-person closing starts that process to developing a dialogue with the seller that is not part of the negotiation. The negotiation is head-to-head, trying to extract the value, almost zero-sum, whereas once you have the closing you can start that dialogue. And you can have a virtual closing anytime, but if you set a date for an in-person closing of Friday, December 30th, for example, it imparts a bit more urgency and seriousness to the negotiations of the Purchase Agreement and the diligence. That's really real."

Van Conway, the investment banker with more than 40 years in the business, lamented the demise of the in-person closing: "That's just kind of too bad. I'm an old-fashioned guy."

Conclusion

The devil is in the details of any M&A transaction. The due diligence process, running parallel to the drafting of the Purchase Agreement, is arguably the most important part of unlocking the value of the deal. The dealmakers in this edition, shared their best practice advice on getting through the process and arriving at a successful transaction – or, in some cases, recognizing when it is time to walk away from the deal. Technology has transformed the diligence process dramatically with the proliferation of virtual data rooms and virtual closings. Yet some lament the passing of the personal, confidence building touches measures that existed in the days of in-person signings and closings. And the closing is not THE END – which we explore in the next chapter.

FOUR

After the Deal

Strategies and Issues for the Day after Closing

Part I. Buyer and Seller Post-Close: The Long Goodbye

A. Post-Closing Issues – Financial and Personal

"If we get involved post-close, it's a sign things have gone really, really bad."
– Miroslav ("Miro") Lazarov, Managing Director, KPMG Corporate Finance LLC

As all-too-many couples have discovered, just because you said "I do" doesn't always mean you do. You fell in love (Chapter 1), got engaged (Chapter 2) and exchanged vows (Chapter 3). Now comes the rest of your time together – for better or for worse – maybe including offspring. So goes the world of mergers and acquisitions.

The post-closing period – it could be 100 days or much longer – is the proving time for the value of the deal. Issues that were not foreseen or disclosed during the due diligence process may appear, prompting buyer and seller to reengage in negotiations, or possibly end up in arbitration or litigation. External market forces may change the business landscape for the new company. Customers and suppliers may demand new contracts or relationships as competitors see opportunities to gain ground. And, according to most of the M&A experts who were interviewed for this chapter – management changes, employee attitudes and work performance present some of the biggest risks of all to souring all the strategy and synergy, the diligence and negotiation and goodwill from the deal's closing.

Something seemingly as simple as a brand name can upset an entire deal, says Miroslav ("Miro") Lazarov, Managing Director in Investment Banking for KPMG Corporate Finance LLC. Lazarov has more than ten years of investment banking experience which includes mergers and acquisition execution, recapitalizations and capital raises, primarily on behalf of clients in the energy, chemicals, homebuilding, recreation and leisure, business process outsourcing and consumer electronics industries.

"From the bankers standpoint, we're pretty much gone [after the closing]," he says. "Typically we might see some issues before closing. But if we get involved post-close, it's a sign things have gone really, really bad."

One of those situations developed in a $100 million strategic cross-border deal in which a European company was seeking to enter the US market by acquiring a well-known company within its industry. "We had a situation where frankly up to day of closing we didn't know the buyer was going to change the name of company," Lazarov says. "We kept asking them before the closing 'Hey guys, how's this going to be handled from a branding standpoint – are you guys going to change the name, or keep the name, or is going to be a division-of?' And they were like, 'We'll figure it out before we get done.' Well, they hadn't figured it out and a week [after the closing] they changed the name – and wiped out the good will associated with that brand."

Lazarov adds: "If the buyer is not working on the transition plan post-acquisition – everything from management, website, PR strategy, employment issues – if they're not working on that post-closing, that's a pretty big red flag for us."

Sean V. Madnani is Senior Director at Guggenheim Securities. Madnani has advised on M&A transactions totaling more than $100 billion in aggregate value. If a transition is going smoothly after a closing, Madnani says, it will be evident in a number of ways. "Targets are hitting the numbers. There's a sense of buy-in from all the employees, as well as new employees in terms of meeting strategic plans that were developed in advance of the transaction. You'll see cooperative activity – joint meetings. A sign of success is when you can walk

"If the buyer is not working on the transition plan post-acquisition, that's a pretty big red flag for us."
~ *Miroslav Lazarov*

into a meeting and not be able to identify which employees came from the acquisition and which pre-dated the acquisition." But if things are not going so smoothly: "One of the first signs is fall off in sales. Or a negative change in sales patterns of the acquirer.

"Another is noticeable signs of employee disengagement – you can see people not showing up to meetings, or working different hours, or you're hearing complaints about people generally, more so than you would otherwise. These are all sort of early signs that there are problems that need to be dealt with. That's doesn't mean there are insurmountable problems, but it certainly means that things are not going smoothly," Madnani says.

B. Issues Vary Depending on the Type of Deal

"The damage has to be significant enough." – David Allinson, Partner, Latham & Watkins LLP

Post-closing issues vary greatly depending on the type of deal, says David Allinson, Partner at Latham & Watkins LLP law firm in New York, who is the global Co-chair of the firm's Mergers & Acquisitions Practice and the former Co-chair of the Private Equity Practice Group and the New York Corporate Department. He has broad mergers and acquisitions experience, encompassing both public and private acquisitions, dispositions, carve-outs, tender offers, going-private transactions, co-investments, joint ventures and general corporate matters, including corporate governance and takeover defense.

"When dealing with a private equity firm transaction or sometimes a company buyer, if they're buying a standalone entity you have a different set of issues than when buying a subsidiary of a public company," Allinson says. "With a financial buyer, they're just buying a company, they're going to completely rely on the operations and management team of that target company, whether it's a whole public company or a subsidiary of a public company." In that situation, he said, the issues that come up post-close really are less about integration as opposed to execution of the business plan. They're expecting the business to do well based on how they valued it."

If the integration results in disparities in the expectations of the valuation, Allinson says that doesn't necessarily result in a dispute. "I would say the vast majority of times you actually don't have a full-blown dispute." Instead of going to litigation or arbitration, the parties will effect a purchase price adjustment, sometimes material, but more often than not less than 5 percent of the purchase price. "In a minority of cases, you do see disputes that can't get resolved by the parties talking to each other and coming to an agreement, in which case they go to arbitration. In those situations it's because the dispute relates to a much larger dollar amount in proportion to the overall value. So there you can see anywhere from 5 to 10 percent-plus of the purchase price changing."

Other disputes may arise over indemnification, Allinson says, giving as an example the owners of a company who sold their business and put some of the purchase price in escrow to be used for post-closing indemnification. "You might find out there was a major customer contract the seller had breached. The buyer goes back and seeks recourse against the seller," he says. "The damage has to be significant enough." He has also seen a "meaningful increase" in the writing of Representation and Warranty insurance [see Chapter 3] in the past two years to cover such potential post-closing landmines. "The price [of Rep and Warranty insurance] has become much more attractive. It used to be above 4 percent of the insurance coverage amount, but now prices are lower, often 2.5 - 3.5% of the coverage amount. It's more affordable and more buyers are willing to use it. It is considered a reliable product where buyers have collected insurance without dispute."

Elizabeth Bloomer Nesvold, Managing Partner of Silver Lane Advisors, an M&A advisory firm specializing in the asset and wealth management industries, has advised on more than 150 deals and valuations over a 24-year span. Her clients differ from most industries in that they are primarily "intangible, people assets" who are making and managing investments for clients. She says in only a handful of cases have post-closing disputes resulted in a purchase price adjustment. "The first litmus test is whether the clients approve of the transaction – so all the clients get to vote," Nesvold says. In some cases a majority of clients must approve, in others 60 or 70 percent. "So going into the consummation of the transaction requires a lot of thinking about client perceptions…The business is the business. You can document all the reps and warranties, but the best litmus test in our intangible space is whether or not the clients approve."

Nesvold says the client consent process generally begins just before the consummation of the deal saying: "That's when the buyer gets to start confirming that the business they think they're buying is at least the business that they'll own within a short period of time." The client consent process may run from 45 to 90 days, typically, depending on the type of fund being acquired. If the clients consent, the transaction closes. If most, but not all, consent, the buyer may ask for a price adjustment. "I've only seen a couple of purchase price adjustments – in one it was a bank that was acquired by another bank and then acquired again by another bank, and then they decided to dispose of part of their business. So it was clients who, every time the bank sold had to go through a client consent process, and by the fourth time, some of them weren't so happy. It was like four transactions over seven years – and we ended up with a purchase price adjustment. I represented the buyer so we knew that was the likely case going into it."

C. Leadership: Who's in? Who's out?

"If the clients start to defect, that's a good warning sign. Danger! Will Robinson!"
– Elizabeth Bloomer Nesvold, Managing Partner, Silver Lane Advisors

In another case cited by Nesvold, a financial services entity acquired a business that they had not been in before. "Then there was a change at the top so the guy who championed the deal was ousted," she says. "The new guy coming in said: 'Why do we own this thing? This is not our core business.' He hires McKenzie. McKenzie comes in and of course validated: 'No, you shouldn't own this thing.'" Within a year there was a subsequent sale to dispose of the questioned assets. "So changing leadership – that's a Number One contributor to the fail rate."

On the positive side, Nesvold says, continued or accelerated growth and stability of the client base are important indicators of the success of a transition. "So, near term in our business, if you did what you said you were going to do for your clients, they'll give you the benefit of the doubt through the client consent process. Beyond that, they watch you and especially if you've got a mutual fund with institutional clients, they'll put you on the 'watch list.' If the clients start to defect, that's a good warning sign – Danger! Will Robinson! – something's about to happen," she declares.

Keith A. Maib, Senior Managing Director at Mackinac Partners, has another uniquely focused perspective on leadership post-closing. Maib co-leads Mackinac's Financial Restructuring, Transaction Advisory and Private Equity practice areas and has spent virtually his entire 30-year career in restructuring and M&A in distressed companies. He normally works one situation at a time, and usually goes into a distressed situation as a C-level officer. He gets called into distressed situations by board members or management "to augment its management team with additional expertise and talent to basically effectuate a financial restructuring and/or a turnaround of the business."

"I don't come in to just execute a transaction," Maib says. "I come in to clean the business up, to dispose of operations that don't make any sense." In the wider world of M&A, the post-settlement period can be six to 12 months, sometimes up to two years. In the distressed world, Maib says the time frame is much shorter – "30-45 days at most." In nearly all cases, the seller will exit the business, for obvious reasons. Says Maib: "Look, in the distressed world there's a high correlation between inefficient, ineffective management teams and distressed companies, as you would expect. So as part of a distressed transaction, usually there are a number of key management changes."

Private equity firms are the predominate purchasers of distressed companies, he adds: "I would say those key management changes as part of a distressed purchase are the most important decisions a private equity firm make that determine ultimately the success or failure of the investment. And in my experience most private equity firms are not very good at this. They're not very good at recruiting and hiring and selecting senior management. They're deal people. They're not operating people." Maib also says the successful private equity firms either engage operating people who have talent, or they use board members who have deep operating experience and know how to vet candidates for C-level positions. However, Maib warns, "When the decision is left solely to the private equity firm and primarily to the transaction team, the risk of those new hires failing, in my view, is very high."

He continues: "In the distressed world the leaders have to modify their behavior…I say to people, 'You didn't just wake up one day and just become distressed. You spent a period of time screwing the business up. You

DEAL NOTES

PlayPower Inc.: a distressed company reinvigorated

PlayPower, Inc., based in Huntersville, North Carolina, is the world's largest manufacturer and marketer of commercial playgrounds. Its products are found at schools, in municipal parks and other places. Prior to 2011 it was owned by a private equity firm and had mezzanine financing that was owned by a large hedge fund and a banking syndicate. The company got into a distressed situation and brought in Mackinac Partners' Keith Maib in 2010 to orchestrate a restructuring.

"I spent the first 9-10 months with the management team reworking the strategy of the business, improving margins, improving cash flow, dealing with liquidity issues, discontinuing certain operations and closing down certain operations," Maib says. "So then you have a business and you say, OK, the value of this business probably doesn't reach to the equity so we need to effectuate a change in control and a recapitalization of the business.

"Oftentimes the old management is continuing forward and carrying a lot of baggage for mistakes that the company made. You've got to deal with that. If you looked at the management team that existed at PlayPower when I went into the company in 2010 and the management team that exists today – and I'm talking about the top 15 executives of the company – it's turned over 95 percent, including every C-level position," he says. In 2011, in connection with the restructuring, PlayPower received $45 million in new capital from Apollo Investment Corporation, which acquired 100% of PlayPower. PlayPower will do about $375 million in revenue in the current year, has operations in the U.S and Europe and Maib continues to sit on the board.

marginalized your supply chain. You marginalized your customer base. You marginalized your talent within your organization. And that doesn't get fixed because you sold the business.' So in my world it's absolutely important that people understand the things that need to be addressed, the timetable it's going to take to address those things and the amount of capital it's going to take to support the business in the meantime."

D. The Closing Balance Sheet

"When key milestones are not just met, but celebrated, those are having a very positive impact because people start seeing that, hey this is working!" – Asish Ramchandran, principal in the Merger & Acquisition Consultative Services practice, Deloitte Consulting LLP

In most deals, 30-90 days after the closing, the buyer presents a closing day balance sheet to the seller. Depending on the purchase agreement terms, one of the parties may have to compensate the other for discrepancies; buyers typically pay sellers while sellers usually insist on downward adjustments to funds in escrow rather than paying out of pocket.

"[There are] always surprises, unfortunately," says Maib. Particularly in the distressed world, he adds, "the biggest distinction is that the seller is going away and therefore reps and warranties aren't valid." Often this is reflected in the price. But Maib says he has also seen a big increase in the use of Rep and Warranty insurance policies, and he should know; he was one of the pioneers in using the insurance dating back to 1999. Says Maib: "They're very applicable to bankruptcy settings because, again, there is nobody to stand behind the reps and warranties. For example, if somebody's got a serious concern about a tax rep, laying that off in an insurance policy on an insurance carrier who is going to be around will solve that problem."

Asish Ramchandran is a principal in the Merger & Acquisition Consultative Services practice of Deloitte Consulting LLP in Los Angeles, with 15 years in the M&A business. He is also the Global M&A and Restructuring Technical Services Leader and a recipient of M&A Advisor's "40 Under 40 Award." Ramchandran has led more than 150 transactions, resulting in more than $4billion in savings and $20B increases in market share. "We're soup to nuts – advisory to implementation, pre-and post-closing," Ramchandran says. "When we look for problems we look for milestones and deadlines getting missed and there being no rational explanation for missing them. In our world we call this 'blueprinting' – when a deal is being done we do a blueprint for the entire deal. In that blueprint we'll identify key milestones that are critical to the success of the deal. If those milestones start getting missed, that is an indication and that something's going wrong."Ramchandran also keeps a keen eye out for employee behavior, saying: "If people are quitting before the bonus period, then you know that there is something's wrong. If they're quitting two months before they are supposed to get a 30 percent bonus, you know something's off – they're so frustrated with the situation that they'd rather quit than stay." Another way to identify disenfranchisement, he says, is a measurable drop in productivity. "You should measure individual team performances against the same quarter the year before – if you see a dramatic movement downward, you know that people are not engaged in the process." He adds that "The Street" is also a good source for indicators on public companies: "Analysts' commentaries, rumors, people talking to each other…where there's some smoke, there's generally some fire."

Then there are the deals that going well or better than planned. "When things are going well, you see people confidently and plainly identifying issues that they think need to get resolved because they are now part of the process," Ramchandran says. "They believe that they can help. So when you see people escalating issues for resolution because they believe that when you take the roadblock out they can increase the speed of the integration – those are signs that things are going well. When key milestones are not just met, but celebrated, those are having a very positive impact because people start seeing that, hey this is working!"

Ramchandran sees post-closing balance sheets differing from pre-closing on a frequent basis. He explains: "The most frequent reason is an economic downturn. It has less to do with the deal itself, it's got to do with the fact that assumptions around the deal parameters changed. As an example, what happened in 2007 and 2008. Or what is happening in the oil and gas space right now with the oil prices plummeting. In the standard M&A deal in oil and gas they weren't necessarily thinking that oil was going to fall by 50 or 60 percent in less than six months. So those are external factors you can't control, or acts of God." Also a factor is hidden costs, which happens frequently in high-tech businesses. "There are product roadmaps that they think are valid but then the customers demand changes so quickly that the product is unsellable," Ramchandran says. Recent examples he cites are wearable devices, such as imitators of the iWatch or Google Glass. "They may be very good devices today but for some reason they don't strike the fancy of the consumer. So they do a deal, the premise is 'I'm buying this company because they've got this new wearable technology,' but it doesn't meet the expectations of the market."

Part II: Integration: the Venus Fly Trap of M&A

A. The First 100 Days

"Increasingly these transition services agreements are very, very important. I think of them as being the equivalent of complicated outsourcing deals." – C. David Goldman, partner and head of the International Corporate Advisory Practice Group, McDermott Will & Emery LLP

Getting a deal signed and closed is never enough. The post-close integration strategy and its execution often make the difference between a transaction's success and failure in terms of value capture. Miscalculations, poor integration plans or external factors result in at least half of M&A deals failing by most estimates. The buyer has to integrate the acquired company into the parent company or make sure it can continue to operate as a standalone business. This is often easier said than done. Examples abound of post-close integration assumptions gone awry.

C. David Goldman is a partner in the law firm of McDermott Will & Emery LLP in New York and head of the Firm's International Corporate Advisory Practice Group (including M&A, Private Equity, Capital Markets and Restructuring & Insolvency). In his 38 years as an M&A attorney he has participated in all types of deals, large and small, public and private. He says the post-closing transitional period varies with the type of buyer – a corporate buyer who is buying for a strategic reason; a corporate buyer who is buying for a new operation or a new geography; a private equity buyer; and a fourth category that MWE sees – the family wealth buyer. "Now there are a number of very large family offices built by wealthy individuals who have created their own captive private equity fund and they're doing private equity type investing but not through (traditional PE) funds," Goldman said. All of these buyer types have very different types of motivations, agendas and issues in post-closing."

As an example of the types of transitional services that may be needed after a closing, Goldman cited a deal he is currently working on – a large international corporate buying a global operation of another large corporate, but taking the buyer into a new but related product line, and in new geographies. "So even though they are in same basic industry – food – there are administrative and operational things that the seller does that the buyer had not done before. Some of those were done by the parent of the seller, and so therefore the buyer will be entering into a 'transitional services agreement' under which for a number of months the seller will continue to provide services on contractual basis. If you think about the different types of potential buyers as I described them – let's take the private equity buyer doing a platform acquisition, or a family doing an acquisition in a new industry – they may not have an infrastructure or IT, or finance, or legal. They may be buying the factories and the salesmen, but that doesn't mean they are buying

"Wealthy individuals... have very different types
of motivations, agendas and issues in post-closing."
~ C. David Goldman

the administrative infrastructure of the seller because the seller may only be selling a division or a subsidiary. So increasingly these transition services agreements are very, very important. I think of them as being the equivalent of complicated outsourcing deals. It's an area in which I think many law firms don't devote enough attention to. They don't treat these agreements as important as they should."

Deloitte's Ramchandran highly recommends the development of a 100-day plan to be put into effect upon the deal's close. "The plan needs to be very well thought out and a very discreet plan with a view to the customers, the employees and the suppliers. So you have a 360 degree focus on all of these, and you actually have a named sponsor to lead the post-merger integration," Ramchandran says. He recommends a senior sponsor who is visible to the CEO to lead the process – "someone within the organization who's highly respected, someone who's an up-and-comer, who's been groomed for a more senior role. You want to put your best people on that job immediately after the close so that in the next 100 days you maintain that momentum and then some more." Other sponsors may be middle management in various divisions or departments such as finance, IT, and/or supply chain.

A real danger during this period, Ramchandran says, is underestimating the competition. "When a deal gets consummated, everybody expects – and the competition expects – that you're distracted. That's when they really start going after your customers, saying 'Hey, this company is in the midst of this internally focused activity – their eyes are not on you. I, on the other hand, only care about you. I want to make sure you get what you want.' Customers are susceptible to it. They are worried about the fallout because they have heard that most M&A deals don't work."

"The best buyers organize the 100 day plan before the closing so that everything is seamless," adds MWE's Goldman. "So they've already been talking to customers, to suppliers, to employees. They don't want to have surprises at all."

DEAL NOTES

The emerging "Family Equity" firms

C. David Goldman McDermott Will & Emery elaborates on what he cited as a growing offshoot of private equity investing – family offices. "It's an area that we care about a whole lot. There are all these terribly rich people today. Wealthy families have traditionally been big investors in private equity funds. They would put their $100 or $200 million into the private equity funds and watch them make money. For three reasons we're seeing less of that. One is the returns on private equity aren't as crazy-wild as they used to be. Two, the wealthy families are getting a little bit tired of the fees being paid to the private fund managers. Three, the private equity funds, when they're doing acquisitions, have an investing horizon of, say, five to eight years. They've got to be in and out because part of their contract with their investors is that they'll be liquid within five to eight years. The wealthy families think a little bit differently. Their time horizon is 100 years – they don't care about the five or seven year thing. They're not looking for liquidity; they're looking for constant cash flow. So the basic theory of the private equity fund doesn't comport with what the wealthy families are thinking.

Also, Goldman said, today's wealthy families today not like the Rockefellers, whose roots trade to the 19th Century. "They may be in the first or second generation of wealth. A guy built a big business and cashed out. He's thinking about what his children are going to do. So a lot of times they're buying businesses so their children and grandchildren have something to do. Also, the fourth generation of Rockefellers may not have an expertise in this industry or that industry. But that guy who sold his business for a billion dollars – maybe he was in the beer distribution business – he probably feels he knows something about distribution so he says I'd like to be dabbling, or investing in this industry and if I just go to a private equity firm, they don't have that particular industry expertise that I have. Or there may be the guy who says he wants to invest the next 20 years in green technology because I really care about that. So the family wealth in my view is migrating away from private equity. They're still doing controlled investments and buying 100 percent of companies, and they're building infrastructures internally that look at lot like private equity funds."

Globally, Goldman said, the recent wealth buildup in emerging markets like China and Russia has also created demand from wealthy families to move assets out of their countries to avoid country risk. Ten years ago, MWE was seeing very little of this activity but today it's a material part of its business, Goldman said. MWE created a separate practice area two years ago. "The reason why we're doing it is because we have what most people agree is one of the top wealth planning practices in the world. So we already represent a large number of these very wealthy families and we understand the kinds of issues that these wealthy families have, whether they're tax issues, succession planning issues, governance issues, all those things that we're dealing with every day. And we also have what most people will accept as one of the top tax practices in the world, which is relevant to these types of investments. And we have a very strong corporate group – private equity group. So combine all those and we have something we don't think other firms have."

B. Post-Closing Issues of Sellers

"The more complicated the earn out and the more complicated the financial metric, that really increases the chance of disputes." – David Allinson, Latham and Watkins.

"Earn outs are the biggest issue for the selling shareholders," says Miro Lazarov of KPMG Corporate Finance LLC. "If you look across the board at probably 50 percent of the companies, the sellers don't end up collecting a portion of the earn outs. Part of that is driven by what kind of metrics you are using for your earn outs. If your earn out is based on EBITA, how is that going to be calculated post-closing? You'll be surprised how many times we've seen deals where's it not really calculated beforehand – it's one of those things where they think they'll just figure it out. The second thing is when you're selling the company you try to put the best foot forward and so you put projections out that in reality don't always happen. Sometimes those projections are not frankly achievable and so the earn outs aren't paid, at least not 100 percent of the earn outs."

David Allinson of Latham and Watkins law firm sees disputes over earn outs correlating to how complicated the earn outs are structured. "Earn outs come in a lot of different flavors," he adds. Common ones are achieving a certain EBITDA threshold in years 2, 3 and 4. Or it could be a revenue test, a contribution test or a growth margin test. "Take EBITDA – you have to agree on what counts and what doesn't count. Those become highly negotiated. And also there's language on how you run the business post-close. The seller's always afraid that the buyer won't operate in the ordinary course and that will impact their ability to get their earn outs. The more complicated the earn out and the more complicated the financial metric, that really increases the chance of disputes."

Lazarov says many merger partners overestimate the synergies that they think will come with a deal. "Things kind of look good on paper or in a PowerPoint presentation. The reality is it takes a lot longer to digest a potential deal or acquisition," he said. On the balance sheet, you shouldn't be seeing anything that's surprising "unless the bankers and accountants are doing their job horribly through the due diligence process," he notes. Or the post-closing balance sheet may be impacted by a sudden change in the economy or the industry. But typically, Lazarov says, there "shouldn't be major discrepancies between what's said before the closing."

In a situation where a public company buys another public company or a division of a public company, Allinson says, the post-closing issues usually relate to operational matters and synergies. "Did the buyer who determined value based on achieving X amount of cost synergies or revenue synergies really achieve it? For a public company it's very important because their valuation, which hinged on those metrics and assessments, usually become public. In subsequent quarters the analysts will ask them how the integration is going, have you been able to achieve those cost synergies. It's important for the public company to explain to the market how they're doing it and how that's reflected in the balance sheet because whether or not they achieve it will start to have an impact on the value of their stock."

Turning to examples of good synergies, Lazarov cited a situation in which the buyer delivered what it promised before the close. "You would think that would always be happening," Lazarov said. "From day one, this buyer had enough trust in the management team they acquired that they actually provided them the budget they needed and new facilities they needed. If you go back and talk to the management team maybe a year later, usually those buyers end up being very happy with the management team they acquired. A lot of my clients are entrepreneurs and with those guys when you're freed up from the day-to-day issues – like being the guy that has to sign off on every bank loan – that's pretty important. So as soon as you remove those bank guarantees, a lot of these guys who might have been building their business the last 20 years all of a sudden are very excited again about really growing and expanding the business."

Another positive example: a company in the oil and gas space. The owners spent 4-5 years building the company before they sold it last year just before the peak of the US oil boom. "These guys built the company literally from zero to $100 million," Lazarov says. "I was talking to them yesterday and they said 'Gosh, we're so happy that now we're part of a publicly traded company because we may have a downturn coming in our industry and we actually – instead of worrying what's going to happen to the company or what's going to happen to the payroll – we can actually take a strategic view of the business five years from now and actually go out and acquire some smaller competitors that are privately owned. So having that support from a larger corporate parent – if it's a nurturing corporate parent – usually means the benefits come down the line."

C. Management Changes – Private and Public

"A lot of time managers who saw themselves as the king of the castle suddenly realize they have someone else to answer to." – David Allinson, Partner, Latham & Watkins LLP

"This town ain't big enough for both of us," the old western movie cliche goes. The M&A landscape is littered with casualties of post-merger management integrations. In the case of private deals – a private equity firm buying an enterprise, managers who founded or ran the business often find themselves in a new situation, with a new board, stringent new reporting requirements and milestones to be rigorously met. The private equity firm usually has a 5-8 year time horizon before it re-sells the business to meet its liquidity obligations to its limited partners.

"They're not public company shareholders who just sit back and look at earnings from quarter to quarter. They are very active managers," David Allinson says. "They themselves are on the board of directors and the will expect management to report up to the board in a way that is not like a public company, it's much more thorough and exacting. So a lot of time managers who saw themselves as the king of the castle suddenly realize they have someone else to answer to, and those people they're answering to own 95 percent of the company. You do see situations where there are growing pains. Good managers get used to it and realize that's the kind of scrutiny they're going to have because that's part of the bread and butter of how they make money."

With public company deals, particularly mergers-of-equals or near equals, the question becomes which management survives? "Before the close you see all kinds of arrangements, the CEO of one company is going to stay. The board may get mixed up – half from one company or three-fourths from one company," Allinson responds. "The winning CEO usually has a dramatic impact who's going to be winning management across the board, but it's not always the case. If you have a merger of equals, there's always a view of who's a little bit more of the acquirer. And if that's not fully accepted, it does create a bad political environment because no matter what, even with a merger of equals, someone's going to have the advantage. And if it's acknowledged that one group is going to be in control, it usually goes better."

KPMG's Lazarov adds: "You've got to be cautious that you're not eliminating some of the talent that you should be keeping on. That's why it's important for your due diligence team to bring in not just the financial guys, but also HR and everybody else that's key in the organization."

Lawyers get involved in these types of management issues, says MWE's Goldman, adding that continuity of management is important to the success of a deal. "Make sure the managers stay on that the buyers want to stay on," he notes. "The types of issues can really sideline a transaction and are relevant to the post-closing period: how much cash are the key management and employees of the seller taking off the table in the deal? And if they're taking out a lot of money, do they have any incentive to stay? So part of the negotiation sometimes is incentivizing the key management to stay. Second, what kind of upside plans will there be for the management who's staying? Increasingly, a lot of the diligence is around post-closing compensation and benefits for the employees so how to deal with that is very important."

D. Other Post-Closing Surprises

"I think the real issues are around people." – C. David Goldman, McDermott Will & Emery

Post-closing disputes make good newspaper headlines but are not as common as they may seem. "Lawyers spend countless hours and pages in a document on how to deal with post-closing claims," MWE's Goldman says. "They do come in a certain percentage of deals. You avoid them by doing really complete diligence – you don't want to be in a post-closing dispute situation. It's no fun. And sellers want certainty – they don't want to find out they sold their business for a certain amount and now they're going to be chased to get some of that back by those rotten buyers forever. Our goal as lawyers on the buy side is to build a structure through diligence to reduce the number of surprises that can come up post-closing."

Buyers and sellers need to think about where surprises may come from: Intellectual Property problems, lawsuits, environmental problems. Goldman adds those are all matters that should be discovered in due diligence. "I think the real surprises come with the people," he added. "Are you getting the people that you really wanted? Are they committed to stay? Are they part of your team? Will they work with you? That's where the surprises come."

Real surprises come up when corporate cultures don't match up – where the buyer expects the management plans to be submitted weekly and management is not used to such scrutiny. "The typical private equity buyer will have its hands in the management," Goldman says. "If the seller's management is not used to that, if they're used to just managing without having 28-year-old experts getting in the middle, that can be a cultural problem. Or if the buyer's a Chinese company and the seller's a US company, there can be cultural problem. So I think the real issues are around people."

Silver Lane's Nesvold notes that management egos can take a significant bruising in the M&A process. "It's often very humbling when you're built this great money management company but then somebody's kicking the tires and wants you to rep and warranty to a bunch of stuff," she says. "This is the part where there's the most angst for our clients. On the sell side, they certainly enjoy the wooing and the courting process where buyers are putting together their proposal and trying to say 'pick me, pick me.' That's the fun part. And then you get to the documentation and you see that first draft – we warn them in advance that it's sort of a humbling process.

"With big egos it's often very difficult to consummate a transaction," Nesvold adds. She's seen cases where the heads of firms "just thought they were the cat's meow. And they never could get to the terms that they felt one should get to for their prestigious empire. And invariably those firms saw erosion because invariably you have to have the next generation of talent team-building. So we've seen cases where the firm could have seen growth with a partner but didn't because an ego got in the way of really listening to the buyer about how they might grow the business."

Part III. Bringing Down the Curtain – and Communicating to Stakeholders

"You don't want to run into the Shakespearean quote 'Methinks the lady doth protest too much.'" – Elizabeth Bloomer Nesvold, Managing Partner, Silver Lane Advisors

The strategies and synergies are agreed to; due diligence is done; purchase agreement and closing – check. What have you done about communicating with your stakeholders? In successful deals, the buyers and sellers begin their communications plan in the very early stages. Part of this is defensive – what if word leaks to employees or customers ahead of schedule. Worse, what if it gets into the media with the wrong messaging?

A good communication plan will capture the "who, what, when, where, why and how" of the deal – the five Ws and the H, as they teach in some journalism schools. The plan will communicate clearly, avoiding complexity and obfuscation. Managers will think of "worst case scenarios," address them and write their messaging points into the plan. At the end of the day, a bad communications plan, a public gaffe by the new CEO, or a not-so-thoughtful post on social media by a company insider could – and have – wrecked the best-conceived deals.

"It's important for companies to understand and define who their stakeholders are," says Guggenheim's Madnani. "I don't think it's always apparent. So – investors, Wall Street analysts, customers, suppliers, employees, the general media, the families of employees – there's a lot of people you could argue are either direct or indirect stakeholders in your company."

Madnani adds that all constituents that will be impacted by the deal need to be reached with "a base message around why it's happening and why it's good. But then too you need a message for each individual constituency and be proactive in the communication so that you're out in front of any issues sooner rather than later with a defined plan of why this transaction happened, what you're hoping to accomplish, how you're going to accomplish it and how you're going to incorporate the interests of those stakeholders.

What not to do, Madnani advises? "If you don't communicate to a certain group of stakeholders, or if you communicate in such a vague or opaque way that they have no clarity as what what's really happening, why it's happening or how it's going to impact them, in the worst case people just shut off or assume the worst."

Silver Lane's Nesvold has seen the good, the bad and the ugly of stakeholder communication. "It's so critical, I cannot emphasize this piece enough," she emphasizes. "In our world [financial services], the first level of stakeholders are younger partners who may not be privy to what's going on until the later stages of the transaction because the majority rules. And so the majority will run through the process. We try to make sure that the right messaging is out there because it's hard to let them know too early because if something doesn't come to fruition, why get people all riled up for nothing? But you have younger partners and employees and anytime you say 'merger' or 'acquisition' the natural instinct is to worry.

"Then beyond that you've the clients and the prospects and the competitive marketplace who will try any bad messaging to their advantage to scoop up prospects or your own clients. So at each phase of the transaction you've got to be mindful of what's the messaging. A lot of times we tell clients early on that we need to think through the public posture statement, and what happens if somebody gets wind, what do you say to somebody? Because if it comes up, you don't want to run into the Shakespearean quote 'Methinks the lady doth protest too much.' 'Oh, no, no, we're not doing anything. We're not going to do anything.' And then you do something and nobody feels happy that you lied to them."

A great deal of prep work goes into a stakeholder communications plan, including drafting of a press release, a key questions and answers document, talking points for the CEO and other spokespeople. Decisions need to be made – who will make the stakeholder phone calls and when? Who will communicate internally with the employees?

"And even if there is no leak," Nesvold says, "it's just a good practice to develop a public posture statement because when the deal happens you're already going to be ready to embrace how you're going to do the messaging when the clients get you on the phone. They want to know that it's good for you, it's good for me. You can't tell them nothing will ever change, and it has to be true because clients, again, will give you a little bit of time but if you lied to them that's a bigger factor for defection. The best answer is 'everything you liked about us we're going to continue to do.' Or 'you wanted to see opportunities for our junior employees; we're going to be able to do that with our new partner.' The messaging is absolutely critical."

Early in her career, Nesvold says, she received some "forced PR training," which taught her a big lesson. A prominent transaction involving two financial services firms in Boston was in the works. "Three weeks before the deal was to be consummated, the Boston Globe put it in the paper. And it turned out the CEO's wife, who knew, told her garden club. So we try to discourage pillow talk."

Conclusion

The M&A Advisor is proud to have presented the "Best Practices of the Best Dealmakers" for a third edition. The art of deal-making continues to evolve and, as we've seen in 2014, show resilience and value to the global economy. This chapter examined the issues that can arise after the close of the transaction, including balance sheet discrepancies, management issues, earn out expectations and computations, and cultural differences – with both positive and negative post-closing outcomes. Finally, we had best practice advice from professionals on stakeholder communication and its criticality. We invite our readers to send us thoughts and comments for further developxment of "Best Practices of the Best Dealmakers."

Déjà Vu

The Return of Antitrust to M&A

Part I: Elections Matter

Elections matter, but not necessarily in ways that can be anticipated. Regarding US antitrust posture toward M&A transactions, the election results of 2008 and 2012 have held true to that axiom. Vibrant in the 1970s, US antitrust actions initiated by the two federal agencies entrusted with that task – the US Department of Justice (DOJ) Antitrust Division and the Federal Trade Commission (FTC) – waned in the 1980s during the Reagan administration, revived during the administration of George H.W. Bush, blossomed during the Clinton Administration, receded somewhat during the George W. Bush administration, and have revived again with President Barack Obama in the White House. In other words, antitrust activity during Republican and Democratic administrations generally appears to reflect the public perception of each political party's traditional antitrust posture: Republican antitrust enforcement tends to be more skeptical of governmental market intervention and places a greater investigative focus on horizontal mergers and price-fixing; Democratic enforcement is more aggressive, with a focus on vertical mergers. Perception, however, often fails to fully capture reality.

According to the prominent antitrust lawyers interviewed for this special report, differences between how Republican and Democratic administrations pursue antitrust cases do exist, but usually those differences are less stark and far more nuanced than is generally imagined. The reason can be found, in part, in the number 95. According to Mark Gidley, who chairs the White & Case antitrust and competition practice, more than 95% of the employees of the DOJ's Antitrust Division and the FTC are permanent and are not political appointees. The fulcrum of DOJ antitrust enforcement strategy necessarily resides in the office of the politically appointed assistant attorney general who heads the Antitrust Division. This person sets the tone in deciding which cases to push, which to settle and which to abandon. "There is more room for policy in antitrust law than in any other area of the law," Gidley explains. At the FTC, which consists of five appointed commissioners, with the majority appointed by the administration in power and the minority belonging to the out party, strategy formulation is reliant on the FTC chairperson and their own policy priorities, and on the commission structure.

While it is true that the US political needle rarely moves more than slightly to the right or left of center, and that radical departures are more myth than fact, it is also true that the confluence of forces beyond the political realm can conspire to produce the illusion that a politically driven radical departure from the antitrust norm has occurred when, in fact, it has not. The antitrust posture of the DOJ and the FTC during the Obama administration is a case in point. While all of our report contributors acknowledge that in general the politics of the Obama administration are to the left of its Republican predecessor and perhaps slightly to the left of its most recent Democratic predecessor, they emphasize that the Obama administration M&A antitrust strategy does not, in the main, represent a sharp departure from historic norms.

So what's different? At first, early Obama administration antitrust policy was designed to help prevent aftershocks of the global financial crisis that was already underway when it took office. Soon, however, other non-political forces emerged that inevitably impacted the administration's antitrust policies in ways that were new and unanticipated. The major apolitical change agent: technology. Technology created the means for economists to create vast computerized simulations – models – of post-merger competitive environments and product pricing pressure. The fuel for these simulations: an unprecedented enormous volume of digitized data. In an attempt to account for this trend and

> *About 95% of the DOJ's Antitrust Division and the FTC are permanent and are not political appointees.*

harness it, in 2010, the DOJ Antitrust Division (in conjunction with the FTC) updated its merger guidelines. While intended to help M&A dealmakers, their attorneys, and the two federal agencies adapt to a new environment, the 2010 guidelines also created consequences that may have been unintended, but which are perhaps combining to alter the M&A landscape for years to come, no matter which political party wins the White House in 2016.

Part II. The Changing Antitrust Landscape: The Political and Legal Backdrop

A. Antitrust: The Origin of the Species

"Speak softly but carry a big stick." – Theodore Roosevelt

Antitrust. For the uninitiated, it is a word fraught with paradox. Who would oppose trust, and what does that have to do with the enforcement of federal government policies aimed at ensuring the appropriate level of competition in industries in the US and, increasingly, around the world? As it turns out, the historical roots of US antitrust enforcement have everything to do with that word. In the late 19th century, trusts were that era's cartels. They were huge and unregulated industrial combinations that dominated American business and drove the economy. Created by business giants named Carnegie, Vanderbilt, Morgan, Harriman, and Rockefeller, among others, trusts set prices, eliminated competition, occasionally ran roughshod over employees and typically dominated the politics of both major US political parties. Abuses endemic to the trust system inspired muckraking journalists and the growth of early labor unions. Trusts also engendered the birth of the Progressive movement in the US and the emergence of an unlikely Progressive flag bearer, President Theodore Roosevelt, a Republican.

In the late 19th century, Roosevelt gained national attention as an aggressive New York City police commissioner, a war hero, a colorful and outspoken assistant secretary of the Navy, an innovative Republican governor of New York and as Vice President of the US in the administration of William

McKinley. In the fall of 1901, after McKinley's death from an assassin's bullet, Roosevelt ascended to the White House. From his days as New York City police commissioner he had befriended muckrakers, imbibing their fury at unfair social and labor conditions and business practices that he was convinced would soon threaten America's social stability, burgeoning prosperity and new global reach. Wielding the 1890 Sherman Antitrust Act as his cudgel, and with the US Supreme Court behind him, Roosevelt almost immediately took on the most powerful industrialist in the US via an antitrust suit: J.P. Morgan.

On February 19, 1902, Morgan was dining at home in New York when the telephone rang. He became enraged when he learned that Roosevelt's Attorney General was bringing suit against Morgan's Northern Securities Company for violations of the Sherman Act. Morgan hung up the phone and muttered to his shocked dinner guests that it was rude to file such a suit without warning. A few days later, Morgan, face to face with Roosevelt in the White House, accused the president of treating him like a common criminal. Roosevelt informed Morgan that no compromise could be achieved in the matter of Northern Securities, and the issue would be settled by the courts.

Morgan asked Roosevelt if any of his other interests were at risk. "Only those that have done something wrong will be prosecuted," Roosevelt replied. In a 2004 speech to the British Institute of International and Comparative Law Conference, DOJ AAG and Antitrust Division head R. Hewitt Pate spelled out the role, practice and continuum of US antitrust enforcement since Roosevelt's presidency:

> Little has changed over the last century in terms of the wording of our antitrust statutes. The Sherman Act was enacted in 1890, the Clayton Act in 1914, and the legislative amendments since that time have been minimal. Yet U.S. antitrust law has come a long way indeed in those years through judicial interpretations of the law. Congress chose not to enact detailed prescriptions for antitrust enforcement, relying instead on the courts to apply the broad statutory principles to particular fact situations. As former Assistant Attorney General William Baxter has observed, this "common law" approach may lack the certainty provided by a more detailed statute, but it "permits the law to adapt to new learning without the trauma of refashioning more general rules that afflict statutory law".[4]
> Our Supreme Court has described the antitrust laws as having "a generality

4. William F. Baxter, Separation of Powers, Prosecutorial Discretion, and the "Common Law" Nature of Antitrust Law, 60 Tex. L. Rev. 661, 666 (1982)

and adaptability comparable to that found to be desirable in constitutional provisions."[5]

US antitrust law began to take shape only when the Supreme Court began to build the basic framework of antitrust analysis in its decisions. In 1911, it decided the landmark Standard Oil case, in which the United States sought to break up the famed oil conglomerate.[6] Observing that the standards of the antitrust law must be developed by the courts deciding each case "by the light of reason, guided by the principles of law and the duty to apply and enforce the public policy embodied in the statute," [7] the Court announced the Rule of Reason, under which the Sherman Act is deemed to prohibit only "unreasonable" restraints of trade. In another decision that year, United States v. American Tobacco Co.[8], involving a conglomerate in the tobacco industry, the Supreme Court emphasized the Rule of Reason's fundamental grounding in competition concerns. This standard proscribed "contracts or agreements or combinations which operated to the prejudice of the public interests by unduly restricting competition or unduly obstructing the due course of trade or which, either because of their inherent nature or effect or because of the evident purpose of the acts, etc., injuriously restrained trade.

Pate later added, "The Supreme Court's pre-1950 decisions set the stage for the late twentieth-century developments in antitrust law. They established the fundamental principle – consistent with the modern approach worldwide – that antitrust laws prohibit only conduct that unreasonably restricts competition, to the detriment of consumers. And the Court established that the type of inquiry required depended on the nature of the particular conduct at issue."

Nevertheless, application of US antitrust law has enjoyed anything but a smooth ride, according to Pate:

> That auspicious beginning did not mean that the course of American antitrust analysis always ran smoothly through the last half of the century. A consequence of the common law approach is that when antitrust thinking veers from the path of promoting consumer welfare, the Supreme Court may follow. We experienced that effect in the 1960s and 1970s as our Supreme Court issued decisions emphasizing artificial presumptions not soundly grounded in economic reasoning. In Brown Shoe, Pabst, and Von's Grocery, the Court ruled that mergers could be found unlawful based

5. Appalachian Coals, Inc. v. United States, 288 U.S. 344, 360 (1933)
6. Standard Oil Co. v. United States, 221 U.S. 1 (1911)
7. Id. at 64
8. 221 U.S. 106 (1911)

on extremely small increases in market concentration.[9] In Schwinn,[10] it abandoned its formerly cautious approach to vertical practices,[11] holding exclusive dealer territories unlawful per se. Similarly, in Albrecht,[12] it held vertical maximum price fixing illegal per se.

As the sophistication of economic analysis increased, our Supreme Court began to re-examine some of these precedents and return to fundamental principles of competition and consumer welfare. In GTE Sylvania,[13] the Court overruled Schwinn, and in State Oil v. Khan, it overruled Albrecht.[14] The Court adopted a significantly different approach to mergers in General Dynamics,[15] refusing to find a violation, despite current high market shares, in a case where those market shares did not reflect a realistic threat to future competition. And in Matsushita,[16] the Court poured cold water on theories of liability that make little economic sense, and it expressed skepticism of liability theories based on price cutting, which is often "the very essence of competition."[17]

Which brings us to 2014 and the crux of the matter: Have political considerations by the Obama administration ushered in a revival of the 1970s? (As an example, the Supreme Court issued 164 written antitrust opinions in 1972, compared to just 81 in 2002.) The consensus among the veteran antitrust attorneys who contributed their insights to this chapter is, no, the enforcement policies of the Obama administration do not represent a sharp departure from the normal continuum. Yet other forces are afoot that may indeed alter the US antitrust enforcement landscape for years to come, regardless of whether the occupant of the White House is a Democrat or a Republican.

DEAL NOTES

War Stories – and Lessons Learned – from the Antitrust Battleground

All are litigators, courtroom warriors whose battlegrounds are the two US antitrust enforcement agencies: the Department of Justice (DOJ) and the Federal Trade Commission (FTC). Two of the litigators have fought on both sides at different stages of their legal careers, currently for corporate clients but earlier on behalf of one or both of the enforcement agencies. Each has war stories.

9. See Brown Shoe Co. v. United States, 370 U.S. 294 (1962); United States v. Pabst Brewing Co., 384 U.S. 546 (1966); United States v. Von's Grocery Co., 384 U.S. 270 (1966)
10. United States v. Arnold, Schwinn & Co., 388 U.S. 365 (1967)
11. See White Motor Co. v. United States, 372 U.S. 253 (1963)
12. Albrecht v. Herald Co., 390 U.S. 145 (1968)
13. Continental T.V., Inc. v. GTE Sylvania Inc., 433 U.S. 36 (1977)
14. 522 U.S. 3 (1997)
15. United States v. General Dynamics Corp., 415 U.S. 486 (1974)
16. Matsushita Elec. Indus. Co. v. Zenith Radio Corp., 475 U.S. 574 (1986)
17. Id. at 594

James Keyte's law firm, Skadden, Arps, Slate Meagher & Flom – Skadden, or Skadden Arps, for short – recently represented creditors during the American Airlines/US Airways merger. He was intimately involved in assessing the antitrust risk and, if necessary, potential solutions, because creditors owned a majority of American Airlines in bankruptcy. In addition to the usual concerns in airline mergers, pricing practices were a significant issue, says Keyte, a partner in Skadden's antitrust and competition practice. "Based on the government's earlier challenge to the H&R Block/Tax Act merger, which hinged in part on the merger allegedly removing a maverick pricer, there was a risk that the government would focus on the possible elimination of US Airways' pricing programs." Yet there were good reasons, in terms of complementary networks and consumer value, for the deal to go through. "We believed that some form of a fix could resolve most of the government's concerns – for enough slot consolidation at DCA was front and center – that other potential problems were manageable and, perhaps most important, that fully litigating the matter in federal court would be very risky for the government." The transaction, he adds, was one of the rare cases where politics may actually have mattered, thanks to strong union support for the deal. In the end, the deal went forward. The combined company emerged from bankruptcy–and the creditors were fully repaid, with interest.

"We are often confronted by deals that raise significant antitrust issues," says David Wales, who leads the Jones Day global antitrust practice. Jones Day represented American Airlines in its successful merger with US Airways last year; he has also been involved in some of the highest profile mergers in recent history, including AT&T/DirecTV, Sprint/T-Mobile, and Reynolds American/Lorillard. Wales, who has the unique experience of serving in senior positions at both the DOJ and FTC, proffers some advice for other antitrust attorneys with less experience: Do not take a passive approach with the antitrust authorities. "Be proactive and strategic in every step of the process," he declares. "Be mindful of the evidence you provide. Be aware of when to offer a fix. Make sure the agencies are put to their proof, because this is an adversarial process, not a popularity contest. Let them know that if they are going to challenge your deal you are willing to fight them in court, if necessary."

Mark Gidley, a former DOJ and FTC attorney who chairs the White & Case worldwide antitrust and competition practice, has two war stories that ended well for him. The first involves the vertical merger of Toyota Industries and Cascade (a manufacturer of forklift attachments), which was challenged by the government. The second involves the SunGard/Comdisco horizontal merger. Both war stories are instructive, ironic, and in the case of the latter, sadly involved tragic circumstances.

Initially, Gidley was convinced the Toyota/Cascade deal would close quickly. However, the same month the deal was announced, November 2013, a DOJ career staff economist generated an unpublished, not-yet-peer-reviewed paper that touched on areas of dispute in the deal – and was then assigned to the Toyota/Cascade transaction. As a result, says Gidley, "We went through the year's biggest vertical scrub." To meet the challenges, Gidley and his team hired the dean of the Yale School of Management, a well-known microeconomist, and in an unusual move, industry experts, including experts in the forklift industry. According to Gidley, the forklift experts, none of whom had Toyota or Cascade ties, told government investigators, "This is an industry with many standards. The standards are public. Anyone who has a good idea can manufacture forklift attachments. There is no patent on these attachments. Market entry is easy." The defense factual work was successful. The DOJ dropped its challenge and the Financial Times named the deal one of the year's most innovative.

In 2001, SunGard Data Systems, one of three companies that dominated the disaster recovery industry, was a Gidley client. SunGard's merger target, Comdisco, Inc., was in bankruptcy. "We struck a deal, on paper, to buy Comdisco, which some thought would reduce the competitors in the disaster recovery to two: SunGard and IBM," Gidley says. This 3-2 result, he recalls, "was too much, even for Republicans." The George W. Bush administration DOJ challenged the transaction.

On September 11, 2001, Gidley was responding to a second request when two hijacked planes hit New York's World Trade Center, resulting in a tragedy that still echoes throughout the political and financial worlds. About 50 White & Case clients lost all their computer systems, including their backups. Gidley said the event of 9/11 appeared to reinforce the government's competition position, necessitating a vigorous response. "We didn't sleep for 22 days. We were working so fast we didn't have time to read the government's exhibits." The White & Case argument: This is not a traditional 3-2 merger; the combined companies will have less than 1% of Fortune 1000 companies as customers because those companies perform disaster recovery on their own. "It was the middle of the night; I was finally reading through the government's exhibits. Government exhibit 72 said exactly what I'd been trying to prove in court. The judge agreed. We were free to close."

Like Mark Gidley, Alan Rutenberg, Chair of the National Antitrust Practice at law firm Foley & Lardner LLP, takes a lessons-learned approach to his antitrust experience. In terms of presenting a market definition perspective, he recommends providing the enforcement agencies with an alternative to their view, one that reveals a broader market with more competitors, saying: "Be able to show what are and are not barriers to entry and that entry has been underway on an ongoing basis." In defending a strategic deal, he says, it is important to present the agencies with a narrative that spells out why the merger parties are doing the deal. "Deals often carry important efficiencies and synergies. If an agency is convinced that a deal might have serious antitrust problems, synergies and efficiencies alone are a heavy burden in proving they will outweigh any harm." Therefore, a clear explanation of a deal's purpose is mandatory, he says: "The information we present, and our explanations must be very fact-specific to the deal, including a description of the role of power buyers and their influence on customer pricing."

B. The Opening Salvo: The Agencies Lay Down Their Markers

"Governmental antitrust intervention will change with elections – to a degree." – Mark Gidley, Chair, Antitrust and Competition Practice, White & Case

Early 2009: In her first speech as Assistant Attorney General in charge of the Antitrust Division of the United States Department of Justice, Christine Varney stated clearly that antitrust scrutiny of M&A transactions would intensify under Obama administration stewardship. Her aim, she said, was to use antitrust scrutiny to help avoid aftershocks from the ongoing global financial crisis. But that wasn't all. She also said that the Antitrust Division would not sit on the sidelines but would instead "push forward" to explore controversial areas of merger enforcement, including vertical theories in which merger parties are not competitors in the same market but instead have a potential customer/supplier relationship or operate in adjacent markets. Like her Federal Trade Commission counterpart, FTC Chairman Jon Leibowitz, AAG Varney entered the post-Inauguration Day fray backed by a team of experienced litigators who were prepared to take to court cases they could win. At the FTC, however, the pro-enforcement majority had begun to beat the enforcement drum loudly even during the Bush administration.

"The enforcement direction will be influenced by elections," declares Mark Gidley, whose long litigation resume includes early-career stints during the administration of President George H. W. Bush handling antitrust issues for the DOJ Deputy Attorney General, and acting as Deputy Assistant AG in the Antitrust Division. "It's always political in the sense that antitrust heads are chosen to reflect the enforcement and policy priorities of an administration," he adds; every incoming administration sets its own antitrust agenda and direction. In every administration, the responsibility for implementing that agenda in an agency in which 95% of the employees are permanent resides with the AAG running the DOJ Antitrust division. In the FTC it resides with the FTC Chairman and the FTC commissioners from the president's party who comprise the agency's voting majority. Yet despite the different backgrounds of the Antitrust Division's AAG and the FTC Chairman and that agency's commissioners, and each party's politically based approach to antitrust enforcement, federal antitrust policy historically has reflected the US body politic, whose needle rarely ventures more than slightly to the left or right of the political center. In other words, radical departures from the established norms are virtually unheard of. Antitrust enforcement during the years of the Obama administration is no exception: its antitrust policies have, in the main, held to those norms. And Gidley points out that the antitrust agencies are very insulated from day-to-day political concerns; career staff attorneys analyze the cases, immune from Capitol Hill.

David Wales, Practice Leader, Worldwide Antitrust and Competition Practice, Jones Day, agrees. Wales, who served as an antitrust attorney at both federal antitrust enforcement agencies during the George W. Bush administration, says it is over-simplistic to claim that political consideration causes dramatic changes in antitrust enforcement. Generally, he says, the Republican version of antitrust enforcement entails less "envelope pushing" by enforcement authorities in pursuit of gnarly cases on the margin. In any administration, he adds, M&A deals that have obvious antitrust issues will be flagged and blocked. The difference between administrations representing rival political parties, he stresses, is on the margin. "Maybe one administration is a little tougher on mergers that are right down the middle. Maybe another administration is more aggressive in its desire to preserve the number of competitors in a specific industry, or more aggressive on the remedy," says Wales, who adds, "I don't think we have seen a huge sea change between the end of the Bush administration and the first few years of the Obama administration."

James Keyte, Partner, Antitrust and Competition, Skadden Arps, attributes some of the Obama administration's increased antitrust scrutiny to a friendly rivalry between the DOJ and FTC. "There is a healthy competition that has developed between the two agencies in terms of litigation success," he remarks. He traces the roots of that rivalry to the DOJ's loss of a high-profile case in 2004, when a federal judge, who sided with Oracle in its proposed acquisition of software rival PeopleSoft, stated in the ruling that the acquisition posed no threat to competition. Meanwhile, the FTC was victorious in two equally high-profile courtroom battles, forcing a settlement that called for Whole Foods to restore competition by divesting 32 stores acquired in its acquisition of Wild Oats and successfully blocking the attempt by CCC Information Services, Inc. to acquire Mitchell International, Inc. in 2009. Through the years since the DOJ's Oracle setback, through a Republican and Democratic administration, the two agencies have become ever more vigorous in selecting cases they can litigate and win in court. "Both agencies look to hire attorneys who can better position a case to trial." Keyte says, adding that not only has this resulted in government staff with more litigation experience, but "it has also resulted in increased threatened enforcement that, in turn, leads to more consent arrangements or even abandoned transactions."

As anticipated after AAG Varney's 2009 speech, the two federal antitrust agencies have more closely scrutinized vertical mergers. Vertical mergers are between two companies producing different goods or services for one specific finished product. The motivation behind most vertical mergers is a desire by the parties to increase synergies and efficiencies. However, in 2010 the DOJ, in conjunction with the FTC, and in an attempt to inject more flexibility into the merger review process, reformulated the guidelines for horizontal mergers for the first time since 1992. Some of the guidelines, explains Alan Rutenberg of Foley & Lardner, have been updated to better reflect what the agencies were already doing in practice. The guidelines, Rutenberg adds, focus more on the competitive effects of mergers and do not look as rigidly at market definition and market share considerations. "The guidelines may be viewed as less rigidly structured and as a more nuanced analysis." Adding flexibility, he says, makes the new set of guidelines more open-ended" than the previous set thus reducing certainty. In addition, he notes, the focus of the guidelines has changed somewhat and may have made the front end a little less objective because it does not look as rigidly at structural characteristics, market definition and market share." In some ways, Rutenberg acknowledges, the guidelines may have reduced the level of specificity. Nevertheless, Rutenberg says he doesn't see any problems emanating from the 2010 guidelines.

Mark Gidley, however, takes a different tack. The Obama administration, like the Clinton administration, has looked more closely at vertical mergers. Gidley views the Obama antitrust approach as potentially more aggressive than Clinton's. After all, Gidley comments, Clinton, as governor of Arkansas, had chaired the centrist Democratic Leadership Conference and had reinvented the Democratic Party to reflect a more conservative southern perspective. Even Clinton-era FTC Chairman Robert Pitofsky seemed to reflect that perspective. "Bob Pitofsky and would pay close attention to vertical combinations, but he didn't bring many challenges." Gidley notes.

Gidley cites the aforementioned case regarding Toyota Industries' recent acquisition of Cascade, a company with $1 billion in annual revenue that manufactures highly sophisticated attachments for many forklift manufacturers, including Toyota. Cascade does not manufacture forklifts and thus did not compete with Toyota. But the Obama administration's DOJ looked closely at the vertical issues in the transaction, as it was a forklift manufacturer buying a forklift attachment maker. A second request followed. "That second request resulted in very detailed (and time consuming) economic analyses." Gidley recalls, requiring six months to resolve the issues the request raised. "This deal would likely not have been investigated during either of the Bush administrations and perhaps not by the Bob Pitofsky FTC during the Clinton administration."

Ironically, it may have been a controversial merger that was not challenged by the George W. Bush administration antitrust agencies that ignited a cyclical blowback during the Obama administration. In the mid-2000's, Maytag, a leading US washer/dryer manufacturer, acquired Whirlpool, a strong US rival. The combination, which the Bush-era antitrust agencies did not challenge despite the near-absence of any other significant industry competitors, foreign or domestic, created a US washer/dryer giant with an 80% market share. According to Gidley, some observers pointed to highly visible transactions, such as Whirlpool/Maytag, with very high market shares in certain product lines as transactions that should have been challenged "to remind everyone that the Antitrust Division still exists, that the cop is still on the beat."

Unlike the Obama administration, which some accuse of favoring the opinions of merger parties' industry rivals during merger reviews, Reagan-era DOJ Antitrust Division head William Baxter took the opposite approach. Baxter, who was responsible for overseeing the court-ordered break-up of the old AT&T into regional phone companies dubbed "Baby Bells," declared, "If the rivals are complaining, then the merger is an efficient one, [and] we ought to approve it." According to Gidley, the "Baxter Rule" holds: "Industry rivals fear a merger because it will likely push them around in the marketplace." In the long run, Baxter felt that bucking rivals' complaints and approving a merger amounts to creative destruction, which is good for consumers and for innovation.

"It's not just whether or deal is challenged or blocked, it's also about how long it will take to get the deal done."
~ David Wales, Jones Day law firm.

Part III: The Rise of the Machines

A: Technology and an Avalanche of Automated Data Change the Game

"The merger guidelines have developed in a way that gives the government much more flexibility to conclude that a merger can harm competition." – James Keyte, Partner, Antitrust and Competition, Skadden Arps, Slate, Meagher & Flom LLP

The DOJ/FTC 2010 horizontal merger guidelines, which some experts insist strengthen presumptions that a merger is uncompetitive, also add new types of technology-driven evidence. These two factors, which are mostly independent of political considerations, have heightened the level of uncertainty among many dealmakers and may interact to alter the M&A topography for years to come, pushing dealmakers to work harder to nudge deals through the agencies' evolving review process.

The 2010 guidelines, which do not address vertical mergers or acquisitions, supersede those issued in 1992 which, aside from some 1997 modifications, had remained unchanged since issuance. The 2010 guideline revisions do not carry the force of law, but instead are intended to reflect the current and ascendant merger review practices of the federal agencies. The current revisions provide detail on several subjects, especially regarding the economic models created by agency economists and used by the agencies to assess the potential anticompetitive effects on horizontal mergers. These merger simulation models, according to the agencies, "need not rely on market definition." The guidelines state that the DOJ and FTC will place more emphasis on economic modeling tests of "upward pricing pressure" (UPP), "which also need not rely on market definition," and on win/loss data and "natural experiments." This approach, in some quarters of the antitrust community, has since opened the federal enforcement agencies to criticism for creating the appearance of relying on market definition when they support a specific enforcement action and disregarding it in favor of other economic simulation techniques that purport to demonstrate a horizontal merger's anti-competitive impact.

Dealmaker uncertainty has also been intensified by the deletion in the revised guidelines of the popular 35% safe harbor provision which presumed that harmful unilateral effects of a horizontal merger would not arise as long as the merged firm had a market share below 35%. This deletion dilutes the significance of the revised guidelines' higher Herfindahl-Hirschman Index (HHI) thresholds. HHI calculations represent a commonly accepted measure of market concentration.

Below are other highlights of the key merger guidelines which reflect the agencies' current philosophy, including a more detailed description of the effect of HHI's upward revision. These highlights appeared in an April 22, 2010 client update prepared by law firm Davis Polk. Briefly, the revised guidelines:

- Downplay the importance of market definition in the horizontal merger analysis, and state that "[m]arket definition is not an end in itself: it is one of the tools that the agencies use to assess whether a merger is likely to lessen competition." In recent years, the government's biggest court losses in horizontal merger cases (e.g., Arch Coal/Triton, Oracle/PeopleSoft, and – at the district court level – Whole Foods/Wild Oats) have turned on market definition issues.

- Place significant emphasis on price discrimination – a price increase for a small subset of vulnerable customers – which may, in some cases, encourage very narrow market definitions comprised only of those customers.

- Upwardly revise the Herfindahl-Hirschman Index ("HHI") thresholds. The revised guidelines state that the agencies will consider markets "unconcentrated" if, after the merger, they have a HHI below 1,500 (an increase from a threshold of 1,000). A market will be considered "highly concentrated" at a HHI of 2,500 or greater (an increase from 1,800). A merger producing (i) an increase of more than 200 HHI points and (ii) a post-merger HHI exceeding 2,500 will be presumed anticompetitive. The new thresholds, however, do not represent a loosening of horizontal merger review standards but, instead, conform the guidelines to the thresholds that the agencies have most often used in practice.

- Contain a significantly expanded discussion of unilateral effects of a horizontal merger, consistent with the interests of agency chief economists. Importantly, the revisions note that, like new entrants into the relevant market, non-merging firms' ability to reposition their products to offer close substitutes for the products offered by the merging firms may deter or counteract what may otherwise be significant anticompetitive unilateral effects.

According to Davis Polk, the practical implications of the revised guidelines overall reflect "a pro-enforcement perspective and an effort to blunt various tools that merging parties have used successfully in the past to defeat horizontal merger challenges. They are consistent with a more activist enforcement policy."

While our legal experts do not necessarily share the Davis Polk assessment regarding the Obama administration's activist enforcement policy, all acknowledge that the technology-fueled flood of automated data, and its selected use in merger reviews, will have an impact on the merger review process and M&A dealmaking in general, although the long-term nature of that impact is as yet unknowable.

B: Technology's Gift: Seeking Certainty

"Dealmakers don't want to do a deal in which there is excessive uncertainty." – David Wales, Practice Leader, Worldwide Antitrust and Competition Practice, Jones Day

Ironically, in their effort to inject predictability and a higher level of exactitude into their merger review calculations and subsequent enforcement decisions, the enforcement agencies' employment of high-tech computerized simulation techniques appears to have achieved the opposite result for M&A dealmakers who seek deal execution certainty, or at least some predictability.

The revised guidelines and an uptick in deal scrutiny, says David Wales, have deprived dealmakers of some of the certainty they seek during the deal execution process and which they have had since the issuance of the 1992 merger guidelines. "Dealmakers don't want to do a deal in which there is excessive uncertainty," Wales remarks. That uncertainty can consist of economic and financial issues as well as antitrust issues. However, the potential for technology-driven increased antitrust enforcement creates higher risk and uncertainty regarding deal completion and timing. Dealmakers need to be able to estimate a deal's duration. For example, a typical review of a case with antitrust issues can require 6-12 months. Suspension of the deal process for that time span can spawn difficulty for dealmakers and may induce them to question the viability of the deal. Says Wales, "It's not just whether or deal is challenged or blocked, it's also about how long it will take to get the deal done."

The proliferation of automated data and its impact on potential agency enforcement decisions is beginning to cast a shadow over dealmaking. According to Mark Gidley, the massive amounts of machine-readable data may have played a role in the government's review of the Toyota/Cascade merger. "Today, more data is automated and there is a feeling in the agencies that the data exists and must then be analyzed." Gidley does not attribute this trend specifically to the Obama administration DOJ and FTC. The trend predates this Administration, but it has intensified with the tremendous explosion of automated data and economic modeling that takes advantage of this new data.

Today's large-scale computer simulations require the input of 20-30 variables, which can include the projected gross margin of all the competitors in a given industry. Changes in assumptions are made based on combinations of variables which are then run through the simulator. The result is the potential generation of millions of outcomes, which are then compiled.

According to James Keyte, the sophisticated computerized evaluation tools now emphasized by the federal enforcement agencies under the revised guidelines can be effective in evaluating scanner data in retail industries and in facilitating more robust elasticity analysis. Yet, the current iteration of the DOJ/FTC models that suggest the anti-competitive effects of merger analysis remain simplistic relative to how sophisticated they may become during the coming years as information technology evolves. In fact, Keyte explains, for the most part they are all variations on older Cournot competition models—which attempt to measure a merger's effect on output capacity—or Bertrand competition models—which measure a merger's effect on price.

C: UPP and GUPPI: the SABRmetrics of Merger Review

"Baseball is the most quantitative of all sports and has an astonishing number of statistics, just like antitrust reviews." – Mark Gidley, Chair, Global Antitrust and Competition Practice, White & Case

SABRmetrics, invented by baseball statistician Bill James, leaves no aspect of baseball unmeasured and uncompared. Explaining SABRmetrics to the untutored or uncaring is a laborious process that is often unsuccessful. Nevertheless, in less than a generation SABRmetrics have come to dominate the decision-making processes of its most elite professional practitioners, while serving as a snooze button for old-school pros and fans who prefer more traditional measurement methods. Quite literally, SABRmetrics (despite their occasional opacity) have been a game-changer. Will the SABRmetrics of antitrust impose the same game-changing result on the agencies' merger review process—and results? It is early yet in the game, and the jury remains out.

Baseball and antitrust enforcement appear to have much in common, especially in their storage and use of enormous databases of numeric data. Companies store information on gross margins, prices for every product, whether their product offerings consist of 300-500 product offerings or tens of thousands. If called for, the government may request a data strip of hundreds or thousands of variables in computer-readable form in order to crunch and analyze those numbers via simulators. The increasing abundance of digitized data is accelerating the appetite for metadata during merger reviews. Mark Gidley opts for a baseball illustration to highlight the scope of the government's data appetite. To him, it's like merging two successful baseball teams in this era of SABRmetrics; as an example, he cites the Yankees and Oakland A's. Says Gidley: "You can smash together the Yankees and A's and overnight they become an overwhelmingly dominant franchise. And the baseball commissioner would give that combination a definitive thumbs down for competitive reasons," all of which would have been available to MLB economists in a flood tide of SABRmetrics.

The 2010 merger guidelines revisions' emphasis on competitor pricing and relative capacity at the expense of market definition, were driven in part by related two acronyms that would be beloved by SABRmetricians: UPP and GUPPI. The Upward Pricing Pressure (UPP) test now administered by the federal antitrust enforcement agencies during merger review that was invented by antitrust economists Joseph Farrell and Carl Shapiro provides an alternative to traditional concentration based tests in merger analysis. In addition to being free of market definition, UPP's appeal to some is in its ease of use: one formula indicates whether a merging company has an incentive to increase post-merger pricing. The UPP test identifies a company's incentive to raise prices post-merger by comparing its incentive to increase prices due to lost competition and the opposing incentive to decrease prices due to cost synergies. Revisions similar to those that established UPP as a prime indicator of a post-merger environment are underway in overseas jurisdictions, especially the European Union.

The Gross Upward Pricing Pressure Index (GUPPI), also a new tool, assesses unilateral merger price effects in markets for differentiated products. GUPPI provides a quick, albeit somewhat crude, measure of UPP. Like UPP, GUPPI does not rely on market definition or concentration. Instead, the index calibrates the value of sales diverted to one merging company's product due to a post-merger rise in the price of the merger partner's product, relative to the revenue lost due to fewer sales of the product with the price increase. The 2010 guidelines do not establish any clear thresholds for what constitutes a high GUPPI as opposed to a low GUPPI or which values are likely to trigger enforcement actions beyond stating, "If the value of diverted sales is proportionately small, significant unilateral price effects are unlikely." The lack of clear thresholds qualified GUPPI and its UPP cousin as SABRmetrics that produce a higher level of uncertainty for dealmakers large and small.

Does GUPPI have any advantages? Yes, say some economists, such as those at Economists Incorporated (EI). A GUPPI advantage is that it can be extended to include potential efficiencies, which reduce the incentive to raise prices, producing downward pricing pressure because the efficiencies increase the margin on each unit of sales lost due to a price increase.

Yet the verdict of EI senior economist Lona Fowdur is less enthusiastic. Fowdur says that, despite its theoretical elegance, GUPPI provides an incomplete estimate of unilateral incentives because it disregards other factors that influence a company's product pricing decision, such as repositioning by non-merging companies, new market entrants and changes in demand.

Furthermore, GUPPI cannot be employed to quantify the extent of post-merger pricing changes, instead merely indicating the change in the merged companies' incentives to raise prices relative to pre-merger prices. That is why, given the limitations of a GUPPI's analysis, the 2010 guidelines specify that the enforcement agencies may complement GUPPI with other evaluative tools, including merger simulation techniques and any other relevant qualitative or quantitative evidence to determine the extent to which unilateral effects would result in reduced competition.

James Keyte acknowledges the sophisticated simplicity in these new tools. A confessed technology Luddite, he is more concerned with the results produced than about how those results are generated. Like other antitrust attorneys, he is worried that these evaluative tools invariably tend to show an effect that, however inadvertently, can create problems for pro-competitive mergers. The reason: When a company merges with any substantial competitor, the government's model will show that there will be a negative effect because a direct competitor has been eliminated. In Keyte's opinion, there is a battle currently underway pitting those who trust the results generated by new evaluative tools against those who place greater stock in understanding the qualitative evidence of the likely marketwide impact of a merger that acknowledges, among other things, customer negotiating power and the likely reactions of current or additional industry players in response to any sustained attempts at anticipative behavior, post-merger. He says that relying on modeling that de-emphasizes market definition and market dynamics in favor of other factors which may be less relevant amounts to a denial of existing case law grounded in real-world competitive decision-making. Fortunately, Keyte adds, courts occasionally eschew some simulator generated results and instead have reverted to the more traditional benchmarks. In the 2011 case in which the government was successful in blocking the H&R Block/Tax ACT merger (and, more recently, the BazaarVoice/PowerReviews merger), the judge's decision was based not on modeling feedback but instead on the court's study of the merger parties' internal documents.

Nevertheless, Keyte anticipates that an increasing number of court decisions may be impacted by simulation results. His advice to dealmakers: be aware of how results gleaned from modeling results may be used and prepare appropriate responses. He confidently anticipates that many decisions will continue to be based on market definition and structure as well as the quality of documents. In the final analysis, he remarks, "If a company has high market shares, a well-defined antitrust market and documents that suggest the proposed merger will lead to higher prices and reduced innovation, the merger will have problems because in that circumstance the law allows the government a presumption of anti-competitive effects." The H&R Block case in particular, he notes, appears to make it more difficult for defendants to rebut those presumptions. He does not discount the indicative significance of UPP, but UPP results should simply alert the agencies about where else to focus in addition to pricing pressure. In court, he hopes old-fashioned qualitative analysis will retain its prominence in the eyes of judges who rule on merger challenges.

Part IV. Size Doesn't Matter: Middle Market M&A and Antitrust

A: Middle Market M&A Deals Won't Escape Scrutiny

"The Division's preliminary investigation in Bazaarvoice's consummated acquisition of PowerReviews was opened after a Division attorney read about the deal in a trade publication." - Leslie Overton, Deputy Assistant Attorney General, Antitrust Division, US Department of Justice

When it comes to antitrust enforcement, middle market M&A transactions are not exempt from scrutiny. "Size doesn't matter," declares James Keyte, though he acknowledges that big, high-profile deals invite more attention. "When the agencies see an antitrust issue, almost no market is too small." If the government finds a set of consumers that are distinct and may, in the agencies' view, be harmed by a transaction, the agencies have the power to hold up those deals, even if a challenge involves only a small part of a much larger deal." Such challenges, he adds, often result in consent arrangements or other agreements that are aimed at resolving the challenge.

By law, M&A transactions under the $75.9 million threshold are classified as non-reportable to the DOJ and FTC, but that does not mean that non-reportable deals are exempt from agency eyeballs. "Merger parties should not assume that because a deal is too small to be reportable that antitrust constraints do not apply," warns Alan Rutenberg. This was confirmed in April 2014 when, in a speech, Deputy Assistant Attorney General Leslie Overton highlighted the significance of non-reportable merger enforcement. According to Overton, between 2009 and 2013, the Antitrust Division initiated 73 preliminary inquiries into transactions that were not reportable under the Hart-Scott-Rodino Act, the 1976 legislation that amended US antitrust laws. During the same four-year period, non-reportable investigations represented close to 20% of all merger investigations of the Antitrust Division. More than one in four of the Division's investigations into these non-reportable deals resulted in a challenge. The FTC statistics are similar. Between March 2009 and March 2012, about one-fifth of all FTC merger challenges consisted of consummated transactions. The good news for middle market dealmakers is that the vast majority of non-reportable transactions do not result in antitrust investigations. Nevertheless, it is clear from the statistics cited by Overton in her speech that non-reportable merger enforcement represents not just a trend, but a new normal in merger enforcement.

According to Overton, DOJ Antitrust Division enforcement officials learn about non-reportable deals in several ways. Agency lawyers and economists closely monitor developments, including non-reportable deals, in their assigned areas of responsibility. As an example, Overton reveals that "The Division's preliminary investigation into Bazaarvoice's consummated acquisition of PowerReviews was opened after a Division attorney read about the deal in a trade publication." She also acknowledges that the Division learns

DEAL NOTES

Anatomy of the Merger Review Process

All are litigators, courtroom warriors whose battlegrounds are the two US antitrust enforcement agencies: the Department of Justice (DOJ) and the Federal Trade Commission (FTC). Two of the litigators have fought on both sides at different stages of their legal careers, currently for corporate clients but earlier on behalf of one or both of the enforcement agencies. Each has war stories.

James Keyte's law firm, Skadden, Arps, Slate Meagher & Flom – Skadden, or Skadden Arps, for short –represented creditors during the American Airlines/US Airways merger. He was intimately involved in assessing the antitrust risk and, if necessary, potential solutions, because creditors owned a majority of American Airlines in bankruptcy. In addition to the usual concerns in airline mergers, pricing practices were a significant issue, says Keyte, a partner in Skadden's antitrust and competition practice

"Based on the government's earlier challenge to the H&R Block/Tax Act merger, which hinged in part on the merger allegedly removing a maverick pricer, there was a risk that the government would focus on the possible elimination of US Airways' pricing programs."

Yet there were good reasons, in terms of complementary networks and consumer value, for the deal to go through. "We believed that some form of a fix could resolve most of the government's concerns–for enough slot consolidation at DCA was front and center- -that l other potential problems were manageable and, perhaps most important, that fully litigating the matter in federal court would be very risky for the government." The transaction, he adds, was one of the rare cases where politics may actually have mattered, thanks to strong union support for the deal. In the end, the deal went forward. The combined company emerged from bankruptcy–and the creditors were fully repaid, with interest.

"We are often confronted by deals that raise significant antitrust issues," says David Wales, who leads the Jones Day global antitrust practice, which has represented American Airlines in its successful merger with US Airways along with other high-profile cases. Wales, who has the unique experience of serving in senior positions at both the DOJ and FTC, proffers some advice for other antitrust attorneys with less experience: Do not take a passive approach with the antitrust authorities.

"Be proactive and strategic in every step of the process," he declares. "Be mindful of the evidence you provide. Be aware of when to offer a fix. Make sure the agencies are put to their proof, because this is an adversarial process, not a popularity contest. Let them know that if they are going to challenge your deal you are willing to fight them in court, if necessary."

about non-reportable transactions directly from marketplace participants. "For example, the Division opened its investigation into Heraeus's acquisition of Minco after steel producers approached the Division to express their concern that the deal would harm competition." Sometimes, she continues, "We learn about non-reportable transactions that raise competitive questions from the merging parties themselves."

B: The Risk of Non-Reportable M&A Transactions

"The risk of some non-reportable deals can be real and substantial." –
Alan Rutenberg, Chair, National Antitrust Practice, Foley & Lardner LLP

Traditionally, the federal antitrust enforcement agencies pay closer attention to strategic transactions than to financial deals. Anecdotal evidence points to an increase in strategic mergers in the wake of the economic trough of 2008-09. The reason for intensified scrutiny of strategic deals? They are often significant high synergies but also typically involve companies in the same industry and, due to industry structure, the size of the merger parties and other industry dynamics, may therefore invite some degree of enforcement scrutiny.

Despite its rhetoric, the Obama administration's scrutiny of reportable and non-reportable transactions does not appear to Alan Rutenberg to represent a marked departure from the Bush administration. "For most cases, the same antitrust principles have applied and the fact-specific nature of merger reviews continues to apply." Even the apparently invigorated scrutiny, investigation and challenge of non-reportable strategic deals, cited by Leslie Overton in her April remarks, represents a slightly amped continuation of a trend that emerged during the Bush administration. Additionally, the uptick in challenges to non-reportable transactions may be another consequence of the agencies' increasing investment in litigation resources and their aggressive deployment in challenges that appear to be winnable.

C: Involve Antitrust Counsel Early

"There is nothing more terrifying for a seller than a blown deal because the seller is then perceived as damaged goods." – Mark Gidley, Chair, Global Antitrust and Competition Practice, White & Case

Deals can be torpedoed for many reasons, including antitrust challenges. Successful antitrust challenges by the government are dreaded by merger parties big and small, but the threat to middle market merger parties may be more pronounced due to the expenditure of time and resources required to cope with an agency challenge, especially a challenge that results in litigation. Whether a transaction is reportable or non-reportable, arranging the involvement of an antitrust attorney can be an effective preventive remedy.

There are several areas in which early engagement of antitrust counsel can be helpful. For instance, antitrust attorneys can provide effective guidance to the parties on careful document creation, thereby avoiding the unintended courtroom consequences of poorly prepared documents should a merger challenge result in litigation. Explains Alan Rutenberg, "The objective is to avoid making inaccurate or exaggerated statements that can be misinterpreted by enforcement authorities." Several recent cases have pivoted in the government's favor due to such misinterpretations. Early engagement of an antitrust counsel can also help provide guidance on deal structure and on information sharing. "There are many ways to structure any necessary information exchange for due diligence so that all necessary information is seen but in a way that reduces antitrust concerns, such as by using a 'clean team'." Rutenberg says. This can be important because information sharing during the deal execution process can become a concern to antitrust investigators later on and can create an unwanted sideshow as part of a merger investigation. Rutenberg tells dealmakers, "When an agency reviewing your transaction documents sees that the parties may have shared information inappropriately or in a way that was not carefully structured, delay and distraction can ensue in addition to potential legal risk."

The contracting process is another area in which antitrust counsel can provide needed support in formulating the content of a purchase agreement, including efforts clauses, assumption of risk, risk disclaimers, termination abilities and a drop-dead date. In a transaction where the potential for antitrust scrutiny exists, the issue of risk allocation can be key. Buyers and sellers may differ on what constitutes an optimal provision, which can be addressed via a hell-of-high-water clause in which the buyer pledges to take all necessary actions to ensure deal completion. On the other side of the equation, buyers often demand provisions in an agreement exempting them from requirements to agree to any divestiture, remedy or restriction on freedom of action in order to get a deal done.

In this era of more intense antitrust enforcement, dealmakers, including middle market dealmakers, are faced with antitrust consideration beyond merger enforcement. For instance, in buying a company buyers may also be purchasing antitrust risk that has nothing to do with the merging parties. In other words, a buyer may be acquiring a party that is already subject to antitrust scrutiny or to an investigation on conduct grounds. The remedy, according to Rutenberg: In addition to trying to seek contractual protection in the deal agreement, buyers should consider conducting due diligence to obtain a better sense of the antitrust risk they may be assuming by proceeding.

To a man, all the contributors to this chapter urge pre-signing front-end analysis of deal completion and timing risks. According to David Wales, that is often easier said than done, especially if a target prefers not to provide the level of access sought by the buyer. However, he says: "We have been very successful in cases where the seller demands significant deal protection, but to get the level of protection sought, the seller must give us full access to its documents and business people so that the buyer can then formulate an independent assessment of the antitrust risk." He has found that sellers prefer to front-load the antitrust risk, while buyers opt to back-load it. Targets with sophisticated antitrust counsel, he says, often insist on deal protection if is warranted, and less sophisticated targets will often demand a hell-or-high-water clause without explaining the reason for their demand. But the best target counsels, he points out, back up that request with evidence and explain why they believe there are antitrust risks. What neither side wants is a dispute about the facts. The best course, Wales says, is to develop a joint understanding of the facts on both sides. Then the parties can independently assess the antitrust risks and decide what level of deal protection to which they are willing to agree.

Despite the uncertainties afflicting dealmakers under the new merger guidelines, dealmakers, including middle market dealmakers, appear to be taking on the additional risk. "Maybe the market has calmed down and other risk variables have improved when it comes to dealmakers determining whether they want to proceed with a transaction," Wales muses. As an antitrust counselor, he says, his responsibility is to provide those middle market dealmakers with as much guidance as possible in terms of assessing the deal completion risk and timing risk to enable them to make a fully informed front-end decision as to whether or not proceeding with a transaction is a worthwhile endeavor.

If a merger lands in litigation, James Keyte says, that the rigors of front-end analysis and careful documentation can pay off. "Typically, the agencies retreat when they realize they can't win a case," he declares. Often, the government reaches that conclusion early in a case. "Sometimes the market definition will cut one way and you then have to demonstrate to the government that the market definition is too narrow and creates an artificially post-merger high market share." If that persuasion tactic is successful, Keyte says, "the government will go away when it realizes that consumers are not at risk."

Part V: Antitrust Goes Global

A: Antitrust Regimes Proliferate Worldwide

"We publish a worldwide merger survey in which we canvas all the jurisdictions outside the U.S. When we began the survey in the mid-90s we canvassed 40 jurisdictions. Today we canvass 190, 140 of which have merger control regimes."
– Mark Gidley, Global Antitrust Practice of White & Case

Merger control regimes multiply exponentially across the globe, keeping pace with proliferating global mergers. The bad news is that merger control regime standards may vary somewhat from jurisdiction to jurisdiction. The good news, though, is that standards harmonization has increased among the world's major jurisdictions to the point where there are no substantial differences between deals on substance. Although there are occasional outlier cases in which one agency arrives at conclusion that differs from another agency, substantial divergence of outcomes is increasingly rare. Yet some differences continue to exist; while the standards of the European Union do not differ radically from those of the US antitrust enforcement agencies, the EU tends to give the views of competitors than do the US authorities. The EU also devotes more attention to non-horizontal mergers than its US counterparts.

There are also jurisdictional differences not only in substance but in process and timing. For instance, the traditional US waiting period for a non-problematic transaction is 30 days. Parties in global deals, however, must calculate how the difference between US and non-US jurisdiction may impact deal process and timing, as they often do. In China, which is becoming an increasingly important merger control regime because of the huge commitment of US and other Western companies to its economy, filings that do not raise antitrust concerns can require waiting period of up to 4-5 months. Fortunately, China is moving to put in place a simplified filing process in an effort to align with norms in other industrialized jurisdictions. Differences in process also exist between jurisdictions. An example: The EU requires that its Form CO, the standard EU merger notification document, be filed first in draft form, followed by a pre-consultation process.

B: Coping with Global Jurisdictional Diversity

"Take a global view." – Alan Rutenberg, Chair, National Antitrust Practice, Foley & Lardner LLP

In order to help his clients understand and help avoid regulatory concerns in global deals, Alan Rutenberg advises them to take a global view early on in the transaction process. He explains that considering the cross-border implications of a transaction early in the process can be important both to understand the deal timing and substantive risks. When it comes to filings in multiple jurisdictions, he encourages a coordinated approach. While there may be a number of local counsel involved in preparing specific findings, the recommended practice is to have an antitrust attorney coordinate the global effort. While the facts matter, and often can vary from country to country, he adds that the coordinating antitrust counsel can play an important role in helping to develop a consistency of approach in areas such as market definition.

James Keyte recommends that the filing requirements and substantive and procedural frameworks of all jurisdictions involved in a global deal be understood at the outset. A strong management hand on the process is necessary early on, focusing on the nuts and bolts of multi-jurisdictional filing requirements, a complex chore in itself.

For Mark Gidley, whose law firm pioneered overseas expansion back in the 1980s, recourse to an outside courts system in non-US jurisdictions is a vital factor in overseas mergers. Such a safety valve exists in the US to handle disagreements with the government. A second factor is deal reporting, which differs by jurisdiction. Some jurisdictions have unwritten guidance requiring an office visit with the appropriate authorities to explain a transaction in advance of a filing, standard practice in the EU. However, Japan, Korea and other non-EU jurisdictions require a multiplicity of filings. The entire overseas deal process must be closely harmonized in global deals, Gidley says. Regardless of the jurisdiction, the goal is always the same: to close the deal without violating the law.

Step one, according to David Wales, is to quickly determine which jurisdictions will be reviewing a deal. The reality of global dealmaking, he points out, is that most non-US jurisdictions maintain enforcement stances that are more aggressive than the two US antitrust enforcement agencies. He cites the European Commission, Germany, China, Australia, South Korea, Brazil and India as some of the aggressive enforcers. The good news is that the US authorities typically set the pace in global deals, especially if the European Commission, the EU's executive committee, is not involved. Some countries, he explains, are resource-constrained and will piggyback on the US enforcement authorities. Usually the strategy for global dealmakers is to obtain US approval first. Nevertheless, he cautions, "You can't ignore the standards of other countries, especially if there are antitrust issues that are unique to a country involved in a deal, because not every deal has global markets."

Despite its sophistication, the European Commission has been the source of many dealmaker headaches through the years, Gidley says. The EC is usually more aggressive in its enforcement decisions and strategies than its US counterparts, a major difference between the two jurisdictions that Gidley expects will continue. Unlike in the US, where merger parties and the government can resort to the court system for a hearing, the EC "can proclaim your merger blocked, with no meaningful, timely court review." Failure to convince EC regulators of a transaction's merits, he says, will almost certainly result in a dead deal.

Despite the controversy swirling around the question of the Obama administration's perceived enforcement activism and the potential of a murky enforcement future thanks to the likely acceleration of computerized merger evaluation tools, the US, compared to jurisdictions elsewhere, remains the light of the antitrust enforcement world.

Conclusion

Do political agendas have an impact on antitrust enforcement? Yes, as they always have going back to the days of Teddy Roosevelt's White House. Will the current trend favoring technology-driven evaluative simulation at the expense of more traditional merger benchmarks continue beyond the Obama era? Yes. Is a return to the aggressive enforcement of the 1970s likely? No. Will the evaluative tools of today and tomorrow inspire dealmakers and their counsel to test the limits of enforcement? Yes. And if the US enforcement agencies wish to challenge a deal, they must still go before a federal court judge and argue that a deal is uncompetitive, which will require the government to fit those traditional theories and rely on the evidence. For its part, the defense will rely increasingly on early, intense and thorough preparation and risk analysis in order to adapt to the enforcement conditions of a changing antitrust environment. After all, merger partners and their antitrust counsel do not wish to be associated with a transaction that is enjoined.

The Rebirth of Investor Activism

From Raiders to Rescuers, A New Generation

Part I: The Short History of Investor Activism in the United States

"IF YOU want a friend on Wall Street, get a dog," Carl Icahn once quipped. At the time his habit of buying shares in a company and picking a fight with management had got him ostracized as a corporate raider and "greenmailer". Oliver Stone borrowed the canine quip for Gordon Gekko, the cold-hearted protagonist of the film Wall Street'.

"Today, Mr. Icahn does not need the dog: his conduct is applauded by such pillars of the establishment as the head of the Securities and Exchange Commission, the main regulator of America's financial markets: Mary Jo White believes that shareholder activism has lost its distinctly negative connotation." – The Economist, editorial, February, 2014

"Everything The Economist says about shareholder activism is wrong"– Headline on a blog published by Stephen Bainbridge, William D. Warren, Distinguished Professor of Law at the UCLA School of Law in Los Angeles, February, 2014.

T he roots of investor activism in the United States trace to the years of the Great Depression. New laws and regulations were enacted (including the establishment of the Securities and Exchange Commission) with an aim at reforming business practices that were seen as contributing to the worst economic calamity of the 20th Century. The first activists were shareholders who thought the new rules were not enough. Their power and influence were limited. In the early days the principal method of expressing displeasure with corporate management was for shareholders to divest their shares – what was known as the "Wall Street Walk."

Following World War II, the primary activists were labor unions and social organizations. Using activism as a bargaining tool, the Association of Independent Telephone Unions (AITU) bought shares of American Telephone and Telegraph (AT&T) in 1949 to fight pension benefit cuts by the company's management. In 1948, a member of the Congress for Racial Equality, James Peck, purchased one share of Greyhound stock to raise the issue of integrating bus seating in the South to the Greyhound management at their annual corporate meeting. That was seven years before the historic Rosa Parks bus boycott that ushered in the Civil Rights movement.

By and large, activism remained more of an oddity until the latter third of the 20th Century, when the technology-driven information age spawned new means of analysis, organization and communication. The successes of the Civil Rights movement and other activist social and political causes during the 1960s gave rise to beliefs that corporations could also be reformed in similar ways. In one case, a federal appeals court upheld the rights of shareholders – a group of medical students – to fight Dow Chemical's production of napalm, a widely reviled chemical weapon used during the Vietnam War. The illustrious Ralph Nader also engaged in proxy battles with General Motors during the early days of his consumer activism in the early 1970s. These cases generated considerable publicity – but not enough shareholder votes to carry the day.

By the 1980s, the rise of institutional investing forever turned the tide in favor of investor activists. The late California State Treasurer Jesse Unruh was a pioneer, serving as a director of the largest pension fund in the country – the California Public Employees Retirement System (CalPERS). The fund was invested in Texaco, which paid a $137 million premium to avoid a takeover by the Bass Brothers (who owned a 9.9% stake). Unruh viewed this as

"In what has become known, depending on your point of view – either the wolf pack or hyena phenomenon – activists can be successful with relatively small stakes." ~ Rodgin Cohen, Senior Chairman, Sullivan & Cromwell

"greenmail," a term that gained favor throughout a decade that also produced the term "corporate raider" to describe some activist investors, as well as "white knights" for investors who would rush in to rescue a company from a hostile takeover. Unruh pushed CalPERS to adopt a corporate governance policy in 1984. Thereafter, instead of passively holding its stock, CalPERS frequently held corporate managements to account through its sizeable shareholdings and outsized influence. Unruh also helped created of the Council of Institutional Investors (CII) to lobby for shareholders' rights – growing it from 20 public and private pension funds to more than 125 today with more than $3 trillion dollars in assets. CII's website boasts that many of its corporate governance policies "once considered radical" are commonly accepted standards today.

With the rise of institutional investors, the focus of activism shifted from social issues to corporate governance throughout the 1980s and into the 1990s. In fact, the US Department of Labor encouraged this trend through its interpretation of the 1974 ERISA law, generally finding that pension plans administered by organized labor had a fiduciary duty to maximize shareholder value, and should use proxy fights when necessary to achieve that end. One of the chief proponents in the Labor Department in the mid-1990s was Assistant Labor Secretary Robert A.G. Monks, who subsequently formed Institutional Shareholder Services (ISS), which has now played a significant role in corporate governance issues for over two decades. By 1992, the rise in institutional investor activism prompted the SEC to revise its proxy rules to facilitate shareholder communication and lower the cost barriers to collective shareholder action.

The beginning of the new Millennium brought end the of the dot-com bubble in the stock market and a mild recession, along with a spate of highly publicized scandals at big corporations like Enron, WorldCom, Global Crossing and Adelphia Communications. Management misbehavior at these and other companies – some resulting in criminal convictions and prison time – produced investor outrage, which prompted another surge in activism. In March 2004, The New York Times reported that the number of shareholder proposals related to corporate governance issues increased from just over 500 in 2001 to more than 900 in 2003. During the same period, a new crop of activists appeared on the scene – hedge funds. By 2005, they had grown to more than 8,000 funds with more than $1 trillion in assets under management. Unlike previous incarnations of institutional investors – mutual funds, pension funds, trust and endowments – hedge funds were difficult to define and notoriously secretive about their investment strategies, owing to minimal registration and disclosure requirements because of their partnership structures; most have fewer than 100 investors and most investors are qualified as "high net worth." Attempts by the SEC and federal lawmakers during the mid 2000s to require tighter regulation of the hedge fund industry generally failed. At the same time, many of the larger public and private pension funds and endowments began to invest in hedge funds because of their growing track record of market outperformance. As the hedge fund industry has continued to grow (pausing and resetting like other markets after the 2008 financial crisis), many hedge fund managers have engaged in investor activism in order to bolster their returns, leading us to today's frenzy of activity.[18]

Part II: Activism Works – Here's Why

"It was not a long ago that the 'activist' moniker had a distinctly negative connotation. It was a term equated with the generally frowned-upon practice of taking an ownership position to influence a company for short-term gain. But that view of shareholder activists, which has its roots in the raiders of the 1980s takeover battles, is not necessarily the current view and it is certainly not the only view." – SEC Chairman Mary Jo White, remarks at the 10th Annual Transatlantic Corporate Governance Dialogue in Washington D.C. in December 2013

Those 1980s takeover battles generated outsized headlines and one outsized movie (Wall Street, of course). And to a certain extent they still generate headlines a quarter of a century later, including some of the original characters like Carl Icahn, and newer incarnations like Bill Ackman of Pershing Square Capital Management. But the reality, participants in this special report for The M&A Advisor say, is hardly as sensational as the headlines may indicate.

---

18. Source note: much of this short history is derived from a course description in Investor Activism at Harvard University, Professors Lucian Bebchuk and Beth Young, Fall 2009.

"Activism is such a broad term," says Edward Horton, Partner at New York law firm Seward & Kissel LLP. "People come to us with this view that activism implies a hostile approach that always ends up going through a very long and expensive proxy battle that's played out on the front pages of the Wall Street Journal. They're looking at people like Ackman and the household names. In my practice, the majority of what we consider to be activist work or activist advice is nothing like that. It's advising people on such mundane things as Section 13 filings, reviewing corporate structures…or more specifically writing letters and advising on the level of discussion they have with companies."

Horton's firm works with clients that are activist funds as well as issuers but the majority of his work, he says, is in fund advisory, which he has been doing for about 10 years. And, yes, the work is increasing.

As to why activism is on the rise, "I think the short answer to that is – it's money," Horton says. "The money's flowing into activist funds and it's significantly greater than it was even three or four years ago. And the institutional investors that are coming into these funds are also of character that I don't think you would have seen even four years ago. I'm talking about pension money coming in here; some of these foreign sovereign funds coming in. So – large amounts of money that previously didn't want to get involved in the activist world are now coming in, in a big way." New money is increasingly coming in because "activism does work – it does work for current investors," Horton adds.

At the New York law firm Sullivan & Cromwell (which dates to the 1870s), most of the work of Senior Chairman H. Rodgin Cohen goes into defending companies from activist incursions. But Cohen agrees that activism does work – at least for the activists. "There have been activists who have been quite successful. In what has become known, depending on your point of view – either the wolf pack or hyena phenomenon – activists can be successful with relatively small stakes. They have huge amounts of money now. There are all sorts of estimates, but activist funds, many people say, are $150 billion or more. They now receive more support from institutional investors – and that's a pretty powerful combination. And the reason the funds have grown so much is – to their credit – their returns, at least for the short term, have exceeded other hedge fund operators and other money managers. So that attracts even more.

"The other side is – over the past 5 to 10 years – so many of the defenses which companies have had in the past have been stripped away in the context of corporate governance demands. Nobody today has an active rights plan...you no longer have classified boards... you often have special shareholder meeting rights...so the defenses against activists are less, their capacity is more and that's what leads to the overall success and rise of the activists."

Rodgin Cohen also wonders if the US market conditions since 2009 – a spectacular rise in the equities market against the backdrop of virtually zero interest rates – has contributed to the current frenzy in activism. "If you're simply in US equities, as most of the activists are, you can expect to do a good job or you should be really in trouble if you didn't. The bottom line – some of them have done very well...but I think you have to look at in a broader sense and say 'If I were going to just invest in US equities, how that would work out?'"

You may not find a more constructive observer of investor activism than Gregg Feinstein, Managing Director and Head of M&A at New York investment bank Houlihan Lokey (which, interestingly, focuses equally on advising issuers and activists). "The stats show that the returns for activist funds have been in the top 25 percent of hedge funds for many years. So it's clearly financially true that activism works," Feinstein says. "And if you look at the assets in hedge funds... it's also obviously working." Feinstein has been in the M&A business for more than three decades; he's been at Houlihan for the past 10 years, and leads its shareholder activism practice. "Houlihan has become a leader in activism on both the defense side and on the activist side," and today's activism is a "new and improved form," he says, adding that since the recent financial crisis, activism has "come back generally in a more academic, elegant and a more powerful way." Feinstein describes the new breed of activists as more analytical and intellectual – many are very quantitative with very specific plans involving spinoffs, split-ups, share repurchases and capital structure. "Many have common themes which result primarily from many years of artificially low interest rates," he says. "So anything that one can turn into a 'bond' or anything that you could borrow for, algebraically, was going to enhance the stock price. So, if Apple is able to borrow at one percent and use that money to repurchase shares, it's going to help the short-term value. If one can trade something that acts like a bond, one can increase value since investors are so yield-hungry now. The government has helped capital to be so cheap that it leads to all these opportunities. We are also again seeing campaigns to sell the company because you have a very strong M&A market."

David E. Rosewater, Head of Activist Group at Morgan Stanley, has been tracking activist trends through a series of surveys that his firm has conducted with the data provider Merger Markets. "Over the last several years you've seen a great deal of success by activists in their investment returns," Rosewater says. "It's been a very successful strategy and that of course attracts people to the strategy. It also generates alpha and that's what investors are always looking for – the ability to generate returns uncorrelated to the market. That has attracted additional capital as well. From there it's a bit like a snowball down a mountain. Success breeds more interest and more interest breeds more opportunities for success."

DEAL NOTES

Activism is Here to Stay: Schulte/Mergermarket Survey

Schulte Roth & Zabel LLP published its fourth edition of Shareholder Activism Insight, a survey conducted in association with Mergermarket, in late 2014. Shareholder activism, clearly, is here to stay, the report concluded. It examines the opinions of activist shareholders and corporate executives broken out into two groups, one based in the US and one in Europe, in an effort to gain insight into the drivers behind activism in each of these markets over the next 12 to 24 months and the underlying sentiment of market participants.

"The dynamics between activists on the one hand and corporate boards and management on the other are, as always, the driver of the level of discourse about company strategy," the report states. "They are also a determining factor in whether situations play out cooperatively behind the scenes or in contentious, public spectacles. The current backdrop is one of continued growth of activism and the burgeoning power of stockholders. Research group HFR, Inc., recently found that four prominent activist funds had grown their funds under management by $9.4 billion in the first half of 2014 to $111 billion gaining more in that period than the previous two years combined. This signal of the expansion of activist coffers is one that companies cannot afford to ignore."

The results of the 2014 survey reflect the continuing rise in the volume of activist campaigns:

- Some 98% of respondents expect an increase, with more than half of those expecting the increase to be substantial.

- Upcoming activity is expected to be driven by hedge funds (60%) and union funds (24%), which is broadly in line with results of the previous survey conducted in 2012.

- The drivers behind the increase in activism are numerous and varied:
  o 37% of US respondents are most likely to cite poor management performance as their primary motivation for seeking changes to corporate boards.
  o 36% cite a desire to improve corporate governance.

- A substantial number see more harm than good coming out of hostile, high-profile activist campaigns. Instead, respondents are more likely to recommend an active dialogue with management (38%) or shareholder resolutions (32%) as the most effective activist strategy.

- European respondents are divided on the number of shareholder proposals that will receive majority support:
  o About one-third of respondents say that fewer than 10% of proposals will be successful this year.
  o Only 12% are optimistic that 30% or more shareholder proposals will be met with majority support. Remaining respondents have more moderate expectations of proposal acceptance rates.
  o European and U.S. respondents are in agreement that communication is key to achieving desired results. Eighty percent of European respondents cite dialogue/negotiations with management/board as the most effective strategy for achieving desired results, while the remaining 20% say the same of shareholder resolutions.

A complete copy of the report can be found online (at this link: http://www.srz.com/files/upload/Publications/SRZ%202014_Shareholder_Activism_Insight_Report_HR.pdf)

Part III: Does Activism Have A Downside?

"The goal of an activist is to create as much disruption as possible at their target company in order to accomplish their financial objectives – at any cost."
– Matthew Sherman, President, Joele Frank

At the beginning of this report we noted the ringing endorsement of investor activism by The Economist in 2014, and a quote from Stephen Bainbridge, William D. Warren Distinguished Professor of Law at the UCLA School of Law in Los Angeles, who wrote that "Everything The Economist says about shareholder activism is wrong". The Economist editorial cited an

"Activist investing is nothing more than hostile M&A on the cheap,"
~ Matthew Sherman

analysis of around 2,000 interventions in US companies from 1994-2007 that found not only that the share prices and operating performance of the firms involved improved over the five years after the intervention, but also that the improvement was greatest towards the end of the five-year period. Bainbridge wrote that the analysis "was done by folks with skin in the game – a deep ideological commitment to shareholder activism, so deep that they set up a Harvard law school clinic to promote it. I'm not saying they skewed their numbers. They are too good scholars to do that. I am just saying that all empirical studies need to be taken with a grain of salt and those by folks with an agenda need a larger than usual grain. (And, yes, I have skin in this game too.)"

The negative effects generally cited against activism boil down to two questions. First, will the long-term effects on companies outweigh the short-term value gains to shareholders (on which the jury is still out)? And how will the disruption that activism can cause internally affect management, employees, industries, customer and communities?

Matthew Sherman is President of Joele Frank, a New York financial public relations and investor relations firm with a large presence in M&A, and in defending corporations against investor activism. He, like others, sees a myriad of reasons for the rise in investor activism in recent years – including the influence of proxy advisory firms like ISS and Glass Lewis. Sherman also sees an outsized role the media is playing in the trend. "I think the media has played a large role here," he says. "Much of the mainstream financial media now has a dedicated activist beat that reports on daily news and developments of the activist investors. And the media now lionizes activist investors, presenting them as agents of change and corporate governance transformers rather than corporate raiders – this is the most telling sign of how far the public perception about activist investing has shifted."

David Rosewater, who has represented both activists and companies, acknowledges the other side of the argument. "I think clearly there's plenty of opinion that shareholder activism can be harmful, depending on the circumstances," he says. As with everything, it's really specific to the situation. There can of course be circumstances involving particular situations where activism could end up with unexpected results. However, most activists, and certainly all the reputable activists, are working with the focus on benefiting shareholders in general and their track record is quite good overall. That's what the board members are supposed to be doing anyway."

H. Rodgin Cohen, whose work is on the defensive side, says: "It's relatively early, I think, to be able to make a definitive judgment on this new wave of activism." As to possible negative effects of activism, he points to a case where an activist forces the sale of a company at a 20 percent premium. "Over one year that's a hell of a good return. The question is, if the company had stayed around for five years and been sold or been around for five years and been independent, would it have returned more to the shareholders over that period of time?" Rodgin Cohen agrees that corporations exist primarily for shareholders, but notes: "They do have other constituencies. How much is there a transfer of short-term wealth to investors at the expense of the employees and the communities that are served? People can speculate about it but I haven't seen the studies that demonstrate one way or another."

Adds Rodgin Cohen: "One of my former partners who unfortunately passed away a few years ago once said 'All deals are hostile – it's just a question of the level of hostility.'"

Sherman points out that today's form of activism has a much lower barrier to entry. "Activist investing is nothing more than hostile M&A on the cheap," he says. "When you think about it, an activist investor can stand on a very large soap box and gain a lot of traction owning only one or two percent of a company." Sherman also cites possible long-term effects as well as effects on employees, customers, and communities as cause for concern. "Activism can have a significant disruptive impact on a company's operations, and in particular, on its employees, customers, and business partners. Employees may become fearful that their jobs are at stake and customers may become concerned that the company may not be able to continue delivering its products. The goal of an activist is to create as much disruption as possible at their target company in order to accomplish their financial objectives – at any cost."

When asked about the negatives of activism, Gregg Feinstein said: "All you have to do is read articles authored by Wachtell Lipton (a New York law firm), who is focusing the market on some of the negatives. I think the argument is really one of short-term versus long-term and whether overall it's helpful. I think it clearly causes managements to evaluate what they might not evaluate on their own or at the same speed and degree."

Part IV: Is Activism Here to Stay?

A: What About Europe?

"The consensus view is there's a fair amount of undermanaged companies in Europe and ultimately you will see this grow." – David Rosewater, Head of Activist Group at Morgan Stanley

Investor activism may be a raging, rising tide in the US, but across the Atlantic it's barely a ripple by comparison. At the M&A Advisor's International Financial Forum at Bloomberg's London headquarters October 22, 2014, Aaron Kirchfeld, European M&A reporter at Bloomberg News, chaired a panel discussion entitled "Activists in the Shadows." The key question posed to the assembled panel of shareholder activism experts was whether the United Kingdom and Europe were about to experience aggressive US-style shareholder activism. The panelists agreed that there are cultural differences that may inhibit some the practices pursued by activist funds in the US But there are other aspects of shareholder and corporate behavior and corporate governance structures in the UK and Europe that suggest that this region is ideally suited for activist funds to play a more active role in seeking to improve shareholder benefits.

The participants in this special report generally agreed with the London panel. They cite cultural differences as well as a plethora of regulatory structures, differing from country to country across the continent, as inhibitors to US-style activism invading Europe in a big way. "It may change a bit because of the success of activism here," says Sullivan & Cromwell's Rodgin Cohen. "But in a number of countries there are a limited number of targets, or they are protected by the government or they are in private hands. For example, in Germany there are a large number of substantial companies that are private and activism is futile at these companies… I think because of the differences in culture, government and owner structures as such I would be surprised if activism would ever be as high in Europe as in the US."

David Rosewater notes that some firm have set up activism offices in London . But he, too, does not see a sudden surge in activism coming to Europe in the near term. "To some extent it's cultural. The markets are smaller. They're generally thought of as more collegial rather than the rough-and-tumble US market view. With the proliferation of activism, it's not surprising that people who view this as a strategy would look around for other low hanging fruit. And the consensus view is there's a fair amount of undermanaged companies in Europe and ultimately you will see this grow. It's certainly there but it will be a slow build."

Adds Houlihan Lokey's Feinstein: "Everyone has expected a migration to Europe. It has not happened in any material way yet. I think it will happen slowly. We've spent some time – we're working on Intercontinental Hotels now, in London – an $11 billion company. Each country has its own rules. They're not all the same. You have to speak the language. And foreign companies don't necessarily appreciate 'people coming over from the US.' You really have to be a lot more elegant, certainly a lot more patient, in Europe. In England for example, you need to be patient, respectful and genteel, and you need to go to the shareholders first."

B: The Absence of Private Equity Firms

"That's not what private equity is looking for – it's a different philosophy of investment." – H Rodgin Cohen, Senior Chairman, Sullivan & Cromwell

Is there a role for private equity firms, who have largely been absent in the latest rise of activism? Participants in this report say not generally because the business model of private is significantly different – PE firm managers generally aim to acquire and firm and operate it with their own team for 5-7 years before selling or going public whereas activists aim to change strategy within a given company in order to enhance value for current shareholders. Says H. Rodgin Cohen: "That's in large part a difference between a short term and longer-term investment horizon. That is not consistent with the activist approach and it's pejorative, but I think not totally off the mark, to talk about instant gratification for the activist. That's not what private equity is looking for – it's a different philosophy of investment."

Adds Feinstein: "If what they want to do is acquire a company, the worst thing they (PE firms) can do is be the activist who catalyzes a sale, because they're going to sell to anyone other than the PE firm because they were the one that 'put them into play.'"

C: Winners and Losers in M&A?

"As a banker, the peculiar thing about activist defense is that you generally make more money if you lose than if you win." – Gregg Feinstein, Managing Director & Head of M&A Group, Houlihan Lokey

Within the M&A industry, who benefits and who loses from the current wave of activism? Participants in this report agreed that service providers, particularly data companies, law firms, proxy service firms and public relations firms benefit from the increase in activism. The big winners? "It's almost a win-win for activists in any scenario," says Matthew Sherman of Joele Frank. "If the activist runs a successful campaign, they've achieved their objectives. If they settle, they can claim credibility. And if they lose, they still attract outsized attention from the media and other investors. In short, it seems that any attention is good attention for an activist." And the losers? Says H. Rodgin Cohen: "I think the negative impact is definitely on the companies that have to go through it – it's an incredible diversion of management time, resources, funds, and so I see a lot of clients who have to spend a lot of money for what ultimately is not a useful purpose. Quite clearly, if you go through a proxy fight, that money that is spent goes to service providers. Personally I would prefer our clients not have to go through this."

Feinstein points out that in some cases, the apparent losers are the biggest winners. "Everyone involved in M&A is helped because of activism. It's been enormously stimulative to M&A. It helps some clearly more than others – Goldman Sachs, who has the most active defense practice, probably benefits the most. The activist side is still in its infancy. As an example, in our activist campaigns that have been publicly disclosed, the investment banks who seemingly lost made about five times what we did. So, as a banker, the peculiar thing about activist defense is that you generally make more money if you lose than if you win. A lot of activist defense assignments are not set up with a commonality of interests because often the investment banker is paid more if the transaction that the activist is suggesting happens than if they can explain why it is not a good transaction."

As a data provider, S&P Capital IQ has created its own team to serve activist investor clients. Pavle Sabic, Director Credit Market Development there describes the services he provides as crucial to analysis by activists in a variety of ways. "Hedge funds look at 13D and F filings. Investment banks use our data, drilling down into the earnings and financials, and from there they have a look at similar companies. There are many different ways you can use data to find opportunities for investor activism."

One more note of interest: In its database, S&P Capital IQ identifies activist campaigns under 9 categories, ranging from "takeover bid" to "non-confrontational communication and engagement." Want to guess which gets better results? Read Pavle Sabic's conclusion in his blog, at the link which follows: http://www.spcapitaliq.com/insights/investor-activism-popular-misconceptions.

DEAL NOTES

Counterintuitive to the Headlines: Small companies are the biggest targets

S&P Capital IQ publishes insightful blogs by its researchers and analyst on a regular basis on the "Insights" page of its website (link: http://www.spcapitaliq.com/our-thinking/insights.html). In January 2015, Pavle Sabic, Director Credit Market Development, offered some interesting – and counterintuitive – perspectives on where most of today's investor activism occurs – in micro and small cap companies.

"In recent years, investor activism has captured media attention and it is clear to see the effect it is having on the markets," Sabic wrote. "For example, Pershing Square Capital Management's activist campaign for Allergan saw Allergan's stock price rise 87.5% from announcement to exit. But that kind of campaign is not always the norm."

Using S&P Capital Investor's activism database, Sabic shined light on two popular misconceptions: 1) big companies are the exclusive targets of activists, and 2) activist campaigns always involve a hostile takeover threat.

In fact the data showed that over the past three years, micro-cap companies have been involved in 474 activist campaigns. By comparison, Large Caps have seen only 20% of that – 96 campaigns.

Sure, you may say, that makes sense because there are far more micro-cap companies than large cap ones. But Sabic drilled deeper into the data and found that microcap companies are far more likely to be involved in a "successful" activist outcome than are large cap companies.

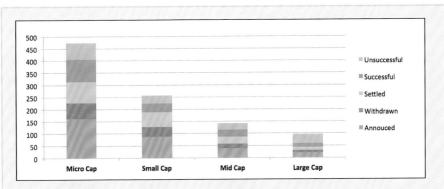

Sure, you may say, that makes sense because there are far more micro-cap companies than large cap ones. But Sabic drilled deeper into the data and found that microcap companies are far more likely to be involved in a "successful" activist outcome than are large cap companies.

Last 3 Years	# Of Successful Campaigns	# Of Unsuccessful Campaigns	Ratio Between Successful To Unsuccessful
Micro Cap	91	69	1.32
Small Cap	35	32	1.09
Mid Cap	28	29	0.96
Large Cap	16	37	0.43

One more note of interest: in its database, S&P Capital IQ identifies activist campaigns under 9 categories, ranging from "takeover bid" to "non-confrontational communication and engagement." Want to guess which gets better results? Read Pavle Sabic's conclusion in his blog (link: http://www.spcapitaliq.com/insights/investor-activism-popular-misconceptions).

D: Here to Stay, but in What Form?

"Overall there probably will be waves of this going forward." – Edward Horton, Partner, Seward & Kissel

Is investor activism here to stay? Participants in this report believe some form of activism will always be around but differ on the timing and extent of the activity. Says Matthew Sherman: "The amount of funds flowing into it speaks for itself and activism today is an accepted form of investment. This has led to a new paradigm in board and management engagement with investors in general. Despite the public perception, many companies and their boards are doing a lot of the right things, notably, maintaining an open and active dialogue with the investment community."

"The only thing that has caused any significant ripple in activism in the last 10 to 15 years was the financial crisis, which affected everybody," says David Rosewater. "Clearly, activist funds were not immune, but not because of the activism component. Value investing has been here forever and activism is really value investing with the activist acting as the catalyst, instead of waiting for the catalyst to occur. Why that should somehow be short-lived is not clear to me."

Supply and demand may be a factor in the level of activism, says Edward Horton: "There are only a certain number of attractive targets, and I don't think it's exhausted, but not every company and not every industry is as attractive to activist holders as others. Overall there probably will be waves of this going forward."

And Rodgin Cohen thinks the markets will be the ultimate judge of the success of today's activist wave. "I think it's here to stay – as long as we have good markets," he says. "How much of the success is due to the policies and pursuits of the activists, and how much is due to an extraordinary bull market. And when the market goes sideways or the wrong way, that's when we'll know. If the activists can continue to prosper through that, it's probably here to stay and if they can't, the real results of it will be demonstrated."

Part V: An Activist Team Has Its Say

A: Meet David Nierenberg and Christopher P. Davis

Most activist investors are unwilling or reluctant to discuss the nature of their work publicly. As noted in the short history of activism, hedge funds have fewer disclosure requirements than do other many other investment vehicles. Thus we are grateful to have had the opportunity and privilege to interview David Nierenberg, Founder and President of Nierenberg Investment Management Company of Camas, Washington, and his trusted counsel, Christopher P. Davis, Partner at the Kleinberg Kaplan law firm in New York.

Nierenberg has been involved in activist investing in two different ways for more than 30 years. In 1985, he left a partnership at Bain Consulting to go into

"Let's face it – what resources does a company have? It has its balance sheet, and it has its off-balance sheet assets which are sometimes process know-how, but most important usually are its people. And if it doesn't allocate them appropriately, it can stagnate or worse." ~ activist investor David Nierenberg

the venture capital business at Trinity Ventures, where he invested in financial services, healthcare and turnarounds. His experience at Trinity included serving on boards of directors of companies the venture firm was invested in. In 1996, he founded Nierenberg Investment Management Company, which manages the D3 Family Funds. D3 Funds investors are "sophisticated" investors that have been in the fund "for decades," and who are typically not institutional investors. The size of the fund is undisclosed. Over nearly two decades, Nierenberg says, D3 has been taken an activist role in about 20 companies that it has invested in.

Davis has two decades of legal experience working with activist investors, including the much publicized Elliott Associates L.P. "We do not do defense work," Davis says. "We are [a] full service counsel to hedge funds. We only represent the activist side of the equation. The fact that we don't represent corporate America has served us well. We don't have the conflicts that some firms who try to walk both sides of the aisle do."

This brings us to how Chris Davis and David Nierenberg found each other. "We used to be a client for many years of a much larger national firm and at one point they decided their job was the defense of corporate America," Nierenberg says. "And even though we believe we approach activism in a constructive and diplomatic way, that law firm fired us because we did not jibe with their mission. So we set out looking for someone who did what Chris did, and as we did our reference checking we were delighted to learn that he had the kind of constructive engagement approach that we think is right for our personality and our style, and we've been working with him ever since."

Nierenberg was asked to explain his philosophy toward activism. His response:

"If you think generically, what are the most important roles of the board of a company, I might say three things: One, to work with management to act strategy and resource allocation program with management. Two, to pick the right chief executive officer to execute that strategy and to oversee the CEO's performance. Three, to set the tone at the top – including having rational, appropriate and fair relationships between performance and rewards.

"Whenever we have been roused to become active in a company it's because we saw something that did not seem right to us involving at least one of those three objectives...This is a small firm and I'm the principal person here that's involved in activism so there's a serious time constraint on the number of campaigns which I can simultaneously pursue. It takes a while."

He further explains that some activists "send out a nasty press release and bash people and play a smash-mouth game – which I've only done once and decided that was definitely not the way I wanted to play the game." Instead, Nierenberg does his homework and meets quietly with management and boards and pursues rational discussion and negotiation. "It is much more time-consuming endeavour because it requires you to establish relations of trust with people with whom you have disagreements about business judgment, and sometimes – rarely, fortunately – but sometimes, disagreements about whether they have conducted themselves properly."

Adds Davis: "There's always the tendency to think of the most recent, high-profile deal and say 'Ah, ha! That's activism!' The reality is that activism has an immense array of permutations. On the one hand, you'll wind up with the nasty proxy fights, litigation, tender offer types of high profile things. On other hand, I think an immense amount of activism, as David says, has been done on a tremendously constructive basis. Activism is at heart value investing. It's finding an undervalued target and trying to find a way to unlock that value. So maybe it is a little more public, unlike how a mutual fund might have approached it behind the scenes, but the goal is still the same thing – make the best company possible, get the stock price up and have the shareholders benefit."

B: A Grain of Sand that Stimulated An Oyster to Make a Pearl

Nierenberg states: "So why is it that boards don't always do those things? Several reasons – the first is oftentimes boards become too clubby, too familiar. You can imagine that any group people who have worked together, often for a long time – even decades – can become comfortable that way. The problem of that comfort is it can stifle questioning, dissent and disagreement. I like to think of the maybe hackneyed analogy – a grain of sand that stimulated an oyster to make a pearl. If no one is in the boardroom asking the kind of question that makes people uncomfortable, then I wonder if that board is actually doing its job. Too often in past, one of criteria for the selection of board members is what I call 'clubbability.' Is this a person that we happen to know socially? Can we get along with this person? So that's one problem – it's really a human nature problem – most people don't like to stand up and dissent.

"The second thing I've observed over the years is that the composition of boards too often reflects where a company has come from, rather than where they're going to. In other words, it may reflect industries, capabilities, geographies, that had a glorious past but may not be relevant to the future. But there seems to be a presumption that once a person is put onto a board, that person will continue serving until they either die, or are disabled or hit a mandatory retirement age, rather than thinking about what skill sets and capabilities does this company need on a going forward basis to be successful, and how does the current composition of the board compare with those requirements and what changes might be appropriate to help the company on its way."

"I'm trying to limit myself to the most common problems rather than the most egregious examples of immoral behavior like back-dating of stock options. I'm trying to be – as I think I am most of the time – empathetic about how it is boards get into this kind of rut. And if they are in that rut, then what are they doing? They may not be making the right decisions about what the strategy of the company should be. They may not be allocating scarce resources of capital and management talent towards driving the growth and value of the enterprise for all stakeholders, and they may not be making tough decisions that need to be made about who should be running the company against what objectives and how they should be rewarded.

"Let's face it – what resources does a company have? It has its balance sheet, and it has its off-balance sheet assets which are sometimes process know-how, but most important usually are its people. And if it doesn't allocate them appropriately, it can stagnate or worse."

C: A Board Indicts Itself In A High Profile Case

Says Davis: "David makes a really good point about the clubbiness of boards, and there's an immensely interesting example that came out just in this last year [Sothebys]… That's exactly what activists worry about. There's this clubby nature that interferes with accountability and that's what the problem is really, I think. And it's pushing the activist movement."

> Wall Street Journal, April 29, 2014: WILMINGTON, Del. — A court hearing Tuesday on a corporate takeover-defense mechanism used by Sotheby's has shined a bright light on discord inside the auction house's boardroom.
>
> The hearing, devoted to the company's use of a so-called poison pill to keep activist investor Daniel Loeb from buying more Sotheby's stock, turned into a public airing of the board's concerns about the company's performance just one week ahead of a shareholder vote to replace three directors.
>
> Lawyers for Mr. Loeb's Third Point LLC read aloud from emails among directors, who privately voiced some of the same concerns he has been raising since October: Sotheby's was overspending, paying its executives too much and falling behind its rival Christie's International PLC.
>
> "The board is too comfortable, too chummy and not doing its job," director Steven Dodge wrote in one email. "We have handed Loeb a killer set of issues on a platter."

"The average hedge fund manager is a fiduciary and has to produce on a consistent basis or money walks out the door," adds Davis. "They're living in a world where accountability is front and center every day, and they look at boards where it's not and they say 'Hold on. You've got our money and you're not doing a good enough job with it.' They're not looking to throw people out for the sake of throwing them out. It's expensive and time-consuming and they've got better things to do. They're looking to make changes so they can get that value returned to shareholders."

Adds Nierenberg: "We focus only on microcap companies, the smallest public companies. The most common issue that I've been working on lately, across multiple companies, is the company that has had a growth vehicle in the past which served it well but which stopped growing for any number of possible reasons. It may have saturated the market. It may have been eclipsed by another technology. It may have been leapfrogged by a competitor. For whatever reason, the glorious engine of the past has started to sputter. And the company may have an installed base, recurring profitable revenue from that business, it may have a strong balance sheet. And so often what seems to happen is that the management and the board treat the financial assets of the company as if their principal purpose is to do everything they can to make the company once again into a growing enterprise.

"The market does like to reward growth more than it likes to reward stagnation, and these people have often grown up in a rapid-growth environment. So they may feel so compelled to find ways to restore the growth that they may simultaneously commence too many growth initiatives without first discerning which of them may be the very, very best, and then metering out the resources for that new growth initiative in a careful, oversight way that a good venture capitalist would do. And they wind up dissipating the financial strength of a company and what's of concern to a value investor like me is that they are using up the margin of safety. And they often wind up making the companies too complex. They wind up with too many simultaneous initiatives; too many to oversee well. And as a result the stagnation may continue or may deepen into a decline."

He continues: "The insiders really need to pull back and do two things. The first is to determine what the very best growth opportunities are, if any exist. And second, they need to think about alternative ways that they might reward shareholders if they cannot resume the growth. For example, think of any kind of national restaurant chain or retail chain that you patronize as a consumer, particularly one that's been growing 20 to 30 percent a year for a long period of time. At some point it will reach saturation, and what will it do then. Well, some companies – those that have a profitable ongoing model – will at that point start to think about using cash to reward shareholders with dividends, or share repurchases to continue providing an attractive total return to the shareholders through all possible means. Or they may even sell themselves. But companies should not assume that continued independent existence while stagnating is their natural right.

"It may well be that there are other outcomes, other strategies, other ways of rewarding shareholders which ought to be considered, even if that may mean that the company may not continue in its core business, the company may not in its independent existence, and – God forbid – some members of the board of directors might lose their prestigious jobs. At the end of the day, what the companies should be trying to do is do right by their stakeholders rather than being a self-perpetuating vehicle for the benefit of the insiders at the expense of everyone else."

D: Is this process like the Five Stages of Grief?

Nierenberg chuckles at the question, saying: "There is something to that. When a business has been good to you for a long time and it stops growing, it doesn't mean that it's a bad business at all. It means that the company should be repositioning for the benefit of stakeholders, rather than say pouring money futilely into growth. And in fairness to the insiders, it is not an easy decision to make. Because if there are ways to make the growth persist in contiguous spaces or other geographies or market segments that the company hasn't penetrated yet, then that's a good thing. The last thing you want to do is walk away from what has been a great cash cow. But it takes good business judgment to decide when enough is enough."

Adds Davis: "You always hear the activists being criticized for following short-term interests – I think that's way, way overblown to the point of being silly – but boards almost never own up to the fact that for many of them, those board positions are incredibly and personally important to them from an economic view. And although they like to pretend that they don't have conflicts, for many of them they do have a conflict, just like when you're dealing in a small or microcap company – or even in some medium-cap companies – the reality is the executives of that company who are desperately holding on – that is likely the very best job they are ever going to have. So being swept out, either in a public fight or a deal where there's a chance of control oftentimes means at least a serious setback, if not a downward trajectory in their career."

Says Nierenberg: "And it can be economic, but it can also be status. It also can be the sense of power and influence that one might attach to being a corporate director. It can be a combination of economic and psychological reasons. But, again, at the end of the day it's not an entitlement. You're there to help the company and help the shareholders."

E: How This Activist Gets Results

"I would say, in the words of Justice Brandeis – 'Sunlight is the best disinfectant,' by which I mean – data is a good thing," Nierenberg says. "It's good to look at historical data of the performance of a company or a business on its own and relatively to a properly constructed peer group, and to look back over the period of time and then answer the question, 'Has this been adding value?' There's a lot of rhetoric that comes from activists, particularly of the smash-mouth variety. I find it much more useful to revert to those three statements of the purpose of the board, and ask people relative to those benchmarks – 'How have we done?' and to look at that through the prism of history and see how the company has done and let the facts speak for themselves. If you do that – look at a relevant peer group – you can often find companies that have pursued other strategies which have produced different results. But generally I find that people do respond to data.

"And I would say that insiders do in one other way as well – they can count. And if they see that there's a certain percentage of the shares of the company that are in the hands of others who are asking the same kinds of questions that I might be, at some point almost anybody can read the handwriting on the wall. So without making yourself into a group, in the legal sense, if enough people are in touch with the insiders asking similar questions, the stubbornness or defensiveness that sometimes exists can be overcome.

"So if I'm looking at a company where I'm thinking about becoming active, one of the first things I'll do is look at the pattern of ownership, to see whether or not the pattern is more or less likely to permit success. As a small practitioner, I have to think about a very important thing to measure which is called 'return on time.'"

Adds Davis: "When a board sees an activist in its stock, one of the first things it will, not surprisingly, do is try to take temperature of its other large shareholders. Nowadays, as say opposed to, say, the 1970s, the institutional ownership is huge as a percentage. So when they go out and start to take the temperature of those other shareholders, or, increasingly, as those other shareholders – even if it's not happening publicly – are starting to reach out to the company to let them know how they view it, that becomes the real important influence as to how the company responds. Even the worst boards can count, and if you're at 60 to 90 percent institutional ownership, and those people for good economic and investment reasons have very similar viewpoints, why are you fighting? Therefore one of the things that other shareholders who aren't activists themselves can do is, if they agree with the thesis, pick up the phone and say so. Sometimes you'll hear allegations of group activity that's not being disclosed. That's incredibly nonsensical – you've just got people who have come to the exact same investment thesis. When people act together, and it happens sometimes, they disclose it and they move on. But you've got a situation in most companies where not surprisingly people can see the writing on the wall. And it's a question of conveying that to the company and the board."

F: How Do You Respond to Critics Who Cite Potential Negative Effects of Activism On Long-Term Performance and on Employees and Their Communities?

Says Davis: "I'm a Delaware law aficionado, so I think the question of other constituencies doesn't come into play. The question is one of the shareholders. And shareholders on the whole are not bothered by activism. The fact that so much money is moving into the space, there are such great returns, is a function of the fact that activism has worked. I agree there's still work to be done but some of the studies that have been done are fairly positive in indicating even three and five years out that companies who have simply gotten on the radar because activists have approached are by-and-large outperforming their peers who didn't have that pressure and that spotlight. Are their failures? Absolutely. No system is 100 percent. It would be very hard to say Bill Ackman's foray into JC Penney was a success. It wasn't. But for every J.C. Penney there are a number of Canadian Pacifics and those turned out quite well."

Nierenberg adds: "You can find legitimate criticisms that can be leveled at activists for both reasons. Again, human nature is in play here. There are as many types of interactive styles as there are personalities. And, yes there are some people in the activist community who act in different ways. I would also note that there board directors, board chairmen and CEOs who handle themselves in different ways. That's the way the world is. And sometimes your behavior as an activist results from what the incumbents have done. In other words, if a management team outright lies to me about something, or does something illegal or immoral – and unfortunately I have to say in 30 years of being on boards I've seen a few of those episodes – then I'm going to act in a much tougher way, in a much more impatient way, than I might behave if I'm dealing with competent, ethical and well-behaving people.

"There is a spectrum of near-term to long-term points of view among activists. Sometimes there can be almost a knee-jerk request when looking at a cash-rich company that it should purchase stock or it should pay a special dividend, and again what's right depends on your best application of business judgment under the circumstances. There is no one-size-fits-all. As I often say to people when they ask me why I'm not asking a company to repurchase stock, for example, the kind of company that should repurchase stock should be a company that not only has the cash to do it, but it should also have a highly profitable business model that the shareholders should want to own a larger percentage of. And the shareholder, through the company's repurchase, should be buying those shares back at a price that is considerably below the intrinsic value. And if those criteria of profitability and value are not met, then a rote response to repurchase shares doesn't make sense. So I think some of those criticisms that are thrown at activists are mirror images of some of the criticisms that activists make at insiders. The devil is in the details," Nierenberg concludes.

Adds Davis: "Not all ideas floated by activists are equal. Nor are they always embraced by the other shareholders. Jamie Dimon survived an activist push quite well because the shareholders agreed with him, not with the activists. There have been several attempts by an activist to get on the board of Cracker Barrel and that has been repeatedly and overwhelmingly rejected. The point about activism, as opposed to the raider activism of the '80s, is this is not about control, it tends to be about ideas and it ultimately comes down to whether the other investors support those ideas or not. And they don't always, but the tendency of shareholders to is really kind of a function of them thinking that the ideas of the activists are pushing are, on the whole, better than the ones management has to offer. The idea that management can say, 'well we've got this plan. It's going to take some time to implement. Just give us another two or three years,' there's really very little patience left with that kind of approach."

Conclusion

The current incarnation of activist investing is a powerful force in corporate governance in America today, with an increasing growth trajectory. The reputation of activists has been transformed from the reviled corporate raiders of the 1980s to the much-applauded new generation of shareholder advocates. Even critics of activism concede that it has produced healthy results for shareholders, although they remain skeptical over whether this is a short-term effect and will be detrimental in the long term. Likewise, critics worry about the distractions that activism puts on even well-managed companies, as well as their employees, customers, industries and communities. While popular and effective in the US, Europe has seen only a small amount of investor activism and the trend is unlikely to catch fire there for a variety of cultural, geographic and regulatory reasons. The only things seem possible to slow activism in the US in the foreseeable future is another economic downturn or, less likely, a severe imposition of regulatory hurdles.

CONTRIBUTORS' BIOGRAPHIES

 David Allinson is Global Co-chair of Latham & Watkins' Mergers & Acquisitions Practice, and formerly Co-chair of their Private Equity Practice Group and New York Corporate Department. He represents private equity firms, including The Blackstone Group, Blue Road Capital, Charterhouse Capital Partners, The Carlyle Power Group, One Equity Partners, and a wide range of public and private companies, including AMC Entertainment, AOL, Cogentrix Energy, and Covanta Holding Corporation. He was recognized in the Financial Times 2013 US Innovative Lawyers Report for his representation of Blackstone Group in its $1.5 billion equity investment in Cheniere Energy Partners, and as a leading lawyer in the 2008 IFLR 1000 guide, The Legal 500 US 2012 and 2008 guide, and Chambers USA 2009.

 Garrett Baker is President at Waller Capital Partners. He initiates and executes M&A transactions for cable and telecom clients, leads cable coverage, and oversees day-to-day operations. Since 2005, Mr. Baker has been the most active M&A banker in cable, representing Wave Broadband, US Cable, Baja & Charter, MCV Guam, Time Warner Cable, The Blackstone Group, and other prominent sales. Previously, he worked at Bear Stearns, and during his career, he's completed M&A transactions valued at over $15 billion-plus. He's been recognized by MultiChannel News as one of the cable industry's "40 Under 40" top executives, and is a member of the Young Presidents' Organization (YPO). He graduated with honors from Wake Forest University, and holds the Series 7, 63, 24 and 79 FINRA licenses.

Mindy Berman is Managing Director and Co-Founder at Investor Group Services IGS. With over 20 years of strategic management, experience, she has led or contributed to hundreds of projects over her career, conducting strategy reviews and industry assessments, overseeing due diligence studies, and developing actionable strategic plans. Formerly a principal at The Parthenon Group, Ms. Berman has a deep resume that includes clients in industries ranging from finance, publishing, and healthcare to industrial machinery, telecommunications, and consumer products. She holds an MBA with distinction from Harvard Business School and graduated summa cum laude from Amherst College with a BA in history.

 Larry Chu is a Partner in Goodwin Procter's Technology Companies, M&A/Corporate Governance and Private Equity Practices, a member of the firm's FinTech Practice, and leads their Technology M&A Practice on the West Coast. His experience includes dispositions, corporate finance transactions, tender offers, carve-outs, asset acquisitions, recapitalizations, buyouts, going-private transactions, joint ventures, strategic alliances, and minority investments in the technology, digital media, financial technology, e-commerce and biotech industries. Mr. Chu has been involved in more than 125 announced transactions with an aggregate value of over $90 billion. He's been recognized as a leading attorney in The Legal 500, and on the Global M&A Network's list of Top 50 North American M&A Lawyers.

 H. Rodgin Cohen is Senior Chairman of New York law firm Sullivan & Cromwell LLP. The primary focus of Rodgin Cohen's practice is acquisition, regulatory, enforcement and securities law matters for US and non-US banking and other financial institutions and their trade associations, and corporate governance matters for a wide variety of organizations. Mr. Cohen and S&C are at the vanguard of critical issues and developments affecting financial institutions, and S&C has long been the firm of choice for leading global financial institutions. Mr. Cohen provides corporate governance advice to a large number of financial and non-financial institutions, both regular clients and as special assignments.

Van Conway is CEO at Conway MacKenzie, nationally recognized for his focus on insolvency/ bankruptcy, financing, reorganization and management of troubled companies, mergers and acquisitions, debt restructuring, and litigation support, across many industries. He's worked closely with debtors, lenders and creditor committees in out-of-court or Chapter 11 restructurings, and consults on turnaround, profit enhancement and cost reduction strategies. A member of many professional organizations, he's a Certified Valuation Analyst, and accredited in Business Valuation and certified in Financial Forensics by the American Institute of Certified Public Accountants. He has a BS/BA from John Carroll University and an MBA from the University of Detroit, has served on several corporate Boards of Directors, frequently writing and speaking on managing troubled companies and litigation support.

Jeff Cox is Senior Partner at Mercer, Inc., where he leads the North America Private Equity M&A Group. He has worked on more than 250 M&A transactions, advising private equity and strategic buyers and sellers on global HR issues, balance sheet risk and post-acquisition integration. Mr. Cox authored the chapter on portfolio purchasing of employee benefits in, The Operating Partner in Private Equity, published by PEI.

Christopher P. Davis chairs New York law firm Kleinberg Kaplan's Mergers and Acquisitions and Investor Activism Groups. He advises domestic and international clients on mergers, stock and asset purchases, shareholder activism, proxy contests and tender offers, restructurings, workouts and bankruptcy sales, stock-for-stock mergers, auction sales, defensive and target reviews, joint ventures, divestitures, financings and minority investments in public and private companies. He has represented investment funds, start-up and mature companies, merchant banks and financial institutions and individuals in general corporate work and in numerous investments, private placements, loans, PIPEs, employment negotiations, Hart-Scott-Rodino filings and business combinations.

James P. Dougherty is Partner at Jones Day. He advises companies on transactional matters, including takeovers, takeover defense, leveraged buyouts, proxy contests, hedge fund activism, and corporate governance. He serves as Administrative Partner for the Global M&A Practice at Jones Day. James has worked on a variety of mergers and acquisitions transactions representing acquirors, targets, and special committees, including Goodrich Corporation in its acquisition by United Technologies ($18 billion); The Lubrizol Corporation in its acquisition by Berkshire Hathaway ($10 billion); Exelis in its acquisition by Harris Corporation ($5 billion); the special committee of Hawk Corporation in connection with its sale to the Carlisle Companies; Nationwide Mutual in its acquisition of Nationwide Financial Services in a going private transaction; and multiple other significant transactions, including spinoffs.

Gene Downing is Co-Founder and President of Downing Wellhead Equipment. Born and raised in Liberal, Kansas, he started as a cement truck driver in oilfield operations. In 1965, he worked for Shaffer Tool Company in Liberal, gaining extensive wellhead equipment experience. In 1971, he was hired by Rector Well Equipment. After years of establishing trusted O&G customer relationships, he founded Downing Wellhead Equipment. Initially specializing in wellhead remanufacturing, they launched their own wellhead equipment brand in 1983. His commitment to quality workmanship, excellent customer service, and rational pricing allowed the company to survive the O&G bust during the mid-1980s. Since then, he's progressively expanded Downing Wellhead Equipment's operations throughout Texas and into North Dakota.

Gregg Feinstein is Managing Director and Head of Houlihan Lokey's M&A Group in the US, Co-Chair of their M&A Commitment Committee, and on the Corporate Finance Board of Directors. He has more than three decades of M&A experience, largely focused on advising publicly traded companies on a variety of matters, including shareholder activism and contested transactions. Mr. Feinstein is based in the firm's New York office. Notable transactions include the hostile takeover defense of Stelmar Corporation, the recapitalization of Trump Hotels & Casino Resorts, the privatizations of Big Flower Holdings to THLee, the activist effort for PSAM to amend the terms of the MetroPCS/T-Mobile merger, and the recapitalization of Samsonite Corporation, which was M&A Advisor's 2003 Middle Market M&A Deal of the Year.

Robert J. Fitzsimmons is Co-Founder and Managing Partner of High Road Capital Partners, a private equity firm formed in 2007 with $470 million of funds under management. High Road is focused on buying and building leading companies at the smaller end of the middle market. As Managing Partner, Fitzsimmons oversees all aspects of the firm's activities. Previously, he served as a Managing Partner with The Riverside Company, as an investment professional with Citicorp Venture Capital, and as a senior accountant with Price Waterhouse. Fitzsimmons has executed over $2 billion worth of transactions over the course of a 25-year career in private equity. He holds a BS in Accounting from the University of Pennsylvania and an MBA in Finance from the University of Chicago.

 J. Mark Gidley heads White & Case's internationally recognized Global Antitrust Group, frequently representing parties in matters with an international dimension. Mr. Gidley served in antitrust-related positions within the US Department of Justice from 1990 to 1993. From 1992 to 1993, he served as Acting Assistant Attorney General for the Antitrust Division. Most recently, he successfully represented Toyota Industries in an acquisition that tested the US DOJ's newly aggressive review of vertical transactions, and Pilot Travel Centers in its Flying J acquisition. The Toyota, Pilot and AnimalFeeds matters each were also designated as some of the Most Innovative US Legal Matters by Financial Times. Mr. Gidley is co-editor of *Worldwide Antitrust Merger Notification Requirements*, a compendium of the merger compliance obligations around the world.

 Simon Gisby is a senior corporate finance professional with over a twenty years of healthcare M&A strategy and investment banking experience. His clients include global pharmaceutical and medical device companies, health insurance companies, hospital systems, physician groups, information technology companies and other healthcare providers. In 2013 and 2014 Mr Gisby was awarded The M&A Advisor Healthcare Deal of the Year He is a frequent contributor to articles and publications on healthcare strategy and M&A and has been quoted in numerous national media outlets. Mr. Gisby is a member of the New York Security Analysts Society, and The Association for Investment Management Research.

Steven Goldberg is Co-Leader of the Baker Hostetler national Mergers and Acquisitions team. He practices in M&A, private equity, general corporate and securities. Consistently recognized in The Legal 500, he was included in the 2013-2015 editions of Chambers USA: America's Leading Lawyers for Business, described as a "master legal technician" and an "extraordinarily bright and hardworking' lawyer who is really adroit at realizing our needs and getting to the core of the issue quickly." In 2015, The Legal 500 named him a "Leading Lawyer" in the <$500 million category. He is the winner of the 2014 and 2012 M&A Advisor TMT Sector Deal of the Year Awards and the 2010 M&A Advisor Middle Market Deal of the Year Award.

C. David Goldman is a Partner at McDermott Will & Emery LLP, leading their International Corporate Advisory Practice Group. Mr. Goldman practices general corporate law and business counseling across several industries, focusing on corporate finance, cross-border and domestic M&A and complex commercial transactions. He has been recognized by Legal 500 as a leader in his field and was selected as "Dealmaker of the Year" by The American Lawyer in 2011 for his representation of Fila Korea and Mirae Asset Private Equity in its seminal purchase of Acushnet's golf business from Fortune Brands Inc. Mr. Goldman is the founder and chairman of the Fellowships at Auschwitz for the Study of Professional Ethics, a foundation that studies contemporary ethical issues in various professions.

Brenen Hofstadter is President and Supervising Principal of Generational Capital Markets, where has spent 20 years specializes in selling privately held companies across the US and Canada. Prior to joining GCM, Mr. Hofstadter was as a partner in a boutique M&A firm specializing in the engineering industry. Earlier, he was Associate Vice President and Managing Director of Citigroup Capital Strategies for 13 years.

Edward S. Horton is a Partner at Seward & Kissel LLP, and focuses his practice on corporate securities law. He's represented domestic and foreign issuers and underwriters in connection with a variety of securities transactions, including initial and secondary registered offerings of equity and debt securities, Rule 144A and Regulation S offerings, private equity investments and other private placements. He also advises domestic and foreign public companies with respect to securities law compliance matters, stock exchange listings and corporate governance matters, and advises institutional shareholders in connection with contested proxy solicitations, activist investing and related matters. Mr. Horton also represents private investment funds and investment managers in connection with a variety of business transactions and securities law matters.

 Villi Iltchev is Senior Vice President of Strategy & Corporate Development at Box, where he leads strategy and inorganic initiatives including M&A and investments. Iltchev most recently was head of M&A at San Francisco-based Lifelock, where he led the acquisition of Palo Alto-based Lemon for $42.6 million. Before that he headed M&A and investment at Salesforce, where he led the San Francisco-based enterprise software company's 2011 investment in Box.

 James A. Keyte is Partner, Antitrust and Competition, Skadden, Arps, Slate, Meagher & Flom LLP in New York. He handles a wide variety of antitrust litigation, transactional and advisory matters. He has led numerous cases involving alleged price-fixing, monopolization, litigated mergers, other restraints of trade and class actions. He's also played significant roles in high-profile matters for the NHL, NFL and the NBA, and has represented numerous clients before the agencies and courts, including the mergers of US Airways/American Airlines, Anheuser Busch/Modelo, Express Scripts/Medco, Coca-Cola/Glaceau. He's the incoming Director of the Fordham Competition Law Institute, and has been selected for inclusion in Chambers USA: America's Leading Lawyers for Business, which has described him as a "brilliant" antitrust lawyer and a "bulldog in the courtroom."

Frank Koranda Jr. is a Shareholder at Polsinelli. Frank assists clients in regard to corporate and financial transactional matters, principally in private mergers and acquisitions. He works diligently with clients to close transactions that further their organizations' goals. Whether a merger, offering, divestiture or financial reorganization, both domestic and international organizations rely on him for strategic legal counsel. He represents private equity and family office backed and strategic buyers and sellers of businesses and product lines. His practice also includes complex debt financings, including senior syndicated and mezzanine financings. In addition to merger and acquisition activity, Frank operates as outside general counsel for a number of private companies, private equity funds and family offices with regard to their merger and acquisition activity as well as the day-to-day management of legal affairs.

Miroslav ("Miro") Lazarov is a Managing Director based in the Orange County office. Miro provides M&A advisory (buy-side & sell-side) and capital structure advisory services to public and private companies in the Energy industry. Areas of focus include upstream, midstream and downstream equipment, services and technologies. Prior to joining KPMG, Miro established the Energy Investment Banking practice for D.A. Davidson & Co. where he specialized in mergers and acquisition execution, recapitalizations and capital raises, primarily on behalf of clients in the oil and gas, power and renewable energy industries. In 2011, Miro received the M&A Advisor's 40 Under 40 Award for his accomplishments in mergers and acquisitions and was also the recipient of M&A Advisor Award for M&A Deal of the Year (2012) and Middle Market Energy Deal of the Year (2010).

Andrew Lohmann is Chair of the M&A Practice at Hirschler Fleischer, headquartered in Richmond, Virginia and winner of The M&A Advisor's "Law Firm of the Year" in 2013 and 2014. His practice focuses on middle market M&A transactions, private equity, corporate and employment law. He is a trusted advisor to middle market private equity sponsors, their portfolio companies and other privately held operating companies. Mr. Lohmann is a three-time national finalist for M&A Advisor's Legal Advisor of the Year Award, earned his BA with Distinction from the University of North Carolina at Chapel Hill (Phi Beta Kappa), and his JD from the University of Virginia School of Law.

Sean V. Madnani is Senior Director at Guggenheim Securities, joining in June 2015 to expand their Investment Banking platform, focusing on technology. He's advised a wide variety of domestic and international clients on M&A, divestitures, spin-offs/split-offs, restructurings, recapitalizations, leveraged buyouts, takeover defense, proxy contests, and capital raising. Previously, he was Partner and Senior Managing Director at Blackstone, leading their Technology M&A practice on the West Coast and Asia. He also worked at Lazard Frères in New York, San Francisco, and London. He received a BA at the University of California, Berkeley, honored as Cal Alumni Scholar and IBM Thomas J. Watson Scholar. He's on the Board of Directors at the Citi Performing Arts Center in Boston, and is a Board Observer at San Francisco's Wingtip.

 Dino Mauricio is a global M&A advisor and Integration/ Separation expert with 20+ years experience as a large-scale Integration consultant, senior investment banker, Fortune 50 M&A leader and private equity investor. He has helped numerous corporate and PE clients achieve world-class integration execution that accelerates growth, maximizes value creation and delivers transformative results. Prior to joining KPMG, Dino held several deal advisory roles– all focused on complex M&A transactions, integrations, JVs and divestitures– including COO and Head of M&A Advisory at Brock Capital, M&A Integration practice leader at Schaffer Consulting, and Head of Transaction Advisory for restructuring firm Getzler Henrich. Dino also held senior M&A leadership roles with GE Commercial Finance, led private equity investments for Berkshire Group and managed Financial Services M&A engagements at LEK Consulting.

 Ron Miller is a Managing Director and a member of the firm's Board of Directors. Mr. Miller has advised clients completing approximately 100 merger and acquisition and public and private financing assignments representing approximately $8.0 billion of transaction value. Prior to forming Cleary Gull in 2002, Mr. Miller was a Managing Director in the Investment Banking Department at Tucker Anthony Sutro, a commercial banker at First Chicago Corporation in Chicago and a Financial Analyst at Morgan Stanley in New York City. Mr. Miller received a M.M. from the Kellogg Graduate School of Management at Northwestern University, a BSE from the Wharton School at the University of Pennsylvania, and a BA in History from the College of Arts and Sciences at the University of Pennsylvania.

Jay M. Moroscak, Esq., is a Senior Vice President with Aon Risk Services based in Cleveland, Ohio. He is responsible for leading client development in the mergers & acquisitions arena. He manages the strategy, client service and development for equity transactions involving private equity funds, strategic investors, venture capital, leveraged buyouts, restructurings, joint ventures & mezzanine financing. Mr Moroscak has extensive experience in due diligence related to risk & insurance issues along with Health & Benefits, Human Capital Consulting and transactional risk solutions, over 15 years of experience in the risk management consulting industry, and in designing insurance programs around his clients' unique needs. He joined Aon Risk Solutions in 2014 and was previously with Wells Fargo Insurance and Marsh.

David Nierenberg is the Founder and President of Nierenberg Investment Management Company, Inc. in Camas, Washington, which manages The D3 Family Funds. Prior to founding Nierenberg Investment Management Company in 1996, Mr. Nierenberg was a General Partner at Trinity Ventures, a venture capital fund, where he invested in financial services, healthcare and turnarounds. Prior to 1985, he was a Partner with Bain & Company, a business strategy consulting firm. Mr. Nierenberg is the Chairman of the Advisory Board of the Millstein Center Columbia University Law School. He is a former chairman of PSA Healthcare. He is also a member of the board of directors at Kuni Automotive Group and Whitman College. He also serves on the Washington State Investment Board.

Elizabeth Bloomer Nesvold is Managing Partner of Silver Lane Advisors. A well-recognized expert in the wealth management industry, Nesvold co-founded the first M&A advisory group for the sector in 1998. Other clients have included trust companies, multi-family offices, institutional and alternative managers, investment counselors, financial planners, investment consultants and financial technology firms. She frequently speaks at investment management industry conferences and seminars, and has authored several articles, including "Who'll Be Left Standing" and "How to Make Money in Wealth Management," for Trust & Estates, and "How to Sell the Family Business (Without Losing Your Sanity)" for Private Wealth Management. She writing her first book for McGraw-Hill on business valuation. She earned a BA from Binghamton University and an MBA from Fordham University Graduate School of Business.

Ben Perkins is a Partner & Senior Managing Director, Life Sciences Mergers & Acquisitions, at Ernst & Young. He has 14 years of lead-, co- and exclusive advisory experience in the pharma, biotech, device, and diagnostic sectors, focusing on equity and debt financings, M&A transactions, and partnership structuring. Mr. Perkins joined Ernst & Young from Merrill Lynch, where he served as a Managing Director leading the West Coast Life Sciences practice. Previously, he served as the Head of Healthcare Investment banking and as a member of the Executive committee for Pacific Growth Equities, a privately held investment bank. He holds a BS from Babson College.

Marc S. Price is an Executive Vice President at Salus Capital, responsible for the structuring of all loan originations and the strategic direction of corporate initiatives. Previously, he focused on asset-based loans as First Vice President, Director of Financial Analytics and Underwriting at First Niagara Commercial Finance. Before that, he was a Vice President at EMCC, Inc., a Schottenstein Stores Corporation affiliate (where he managed their Valuation Services group, and was a member of the EMCC debt-buying investment team), a principal at State Street Global Advisors, and an Associate at General Catalyst Partners, a Boston based Venture Capital fund. He is a member of the Turnaround Management Association (TMA) and Commercial Finance Association (CFA).

Asish Ramchandran is a Principal in the Merger & Acquisition Consultative Services practice of Deloitte Consulting LLP. He is also the Global M&A and Restructuring Technical Services Leader and been recognized as a recipient of M&A Advisor's 40 Under 40 Award. He has led 150+ transactions and has extensive transformation, integration, divestiture, carve-out, spin-off, JV's, restructuring, and technical management leadership experience resulting in $4B+ savings, $20B+ increase in market share.

David E. Rosewater is Head of Activist Group at Morgan Stanley. Previously David was a Partner in the New York office of Schulte Roth & Zabel LLP, where his practice focused on mergers & acquisitions, private equity/leveraged buyouts, distressed investments and acquisitions, and shareholder activism. While his practice spaned numerous industries, he had a particular focus on the financial institutions sector, where he had represented numerous private equity investors in acquisitions or investments involving banks and other licensed financial service providers, as well as representing financial institutions on strategic deals. In addition, as the co-head of SRZ's global Shareholder Activism Group, he had represented companies and shareholders in connection with numerous major shareholder activism campaigns and was named a "Dealmaker of the Year" by The American Lawyer in 2014 for his preeminence in this area.

Alan D. Rutenberg is a Partner in the Washington, DC office of Foley & Lardner LLP and chairs the firm's national Antitrust Practice Group. For more than two decades, he's advised clients in hundreds of M&A matters and multibillion-dollar transactions. He regularly represents clients before the Federal Trade Commission and the Antitrust Division of the Department of Justice on mergers and acquisitions investigations with experience involves managing every phase of the investigation and covering a wide range of industries. He also provides day-to-day antitrust counseling to businesses, litigates antitrust matters, represents clients in conduct investigations by the antitrust agencies, and provides antitrust compliance assistance, litigation, counseling, and training. Mr. Rutenberg graduated cum laude from Harvard Law.

Pavle Sabic is a Director on the Market Development team in the Product & Content division of S&P Capital IQ, focusing on thought leadership and global business development. Frequently published in digital and print media, he presents at industry conferences internationally. He focuses on business development in Europe, the Middle East and Africa. Previously, Mr. Sabic was a product specialist in the risk management division of State Street Investment Analytics, and began his career at Kames Capital. He graduated with a degree in mathematics and economics from Herriot-Watt University in Edinburgh, and holds an MSC from the University of Edinburgh. He has an FRM certification from the Global Association of Risk Professionals, and holds a 40 Under 40 Award for research from the M&A Advisor.

Matthew Sherman is a Founding Member and President of Joele Frank, a financial public relations consultancy in New York with more than 18 years of experience providing strategic corporate, financial and crisis communications counsel to Boards of Directors and executive leadership of public corporations and private equity firms involved in M&A, hostile takeovers, proxy contests, shareholder activism defense, spin-offs, reorganizations, financial restructurings, management changes, litigation, regulatory actions and a wide range of corporate crises.

 Cathy Skala is Vice President/Integration at Baxter International, Inc., in Deerfield, Illinois. Her diverse career started out in commercial architecture, and after several years, she moved into IT, working for several healthcare companies. Her third career change moved her to M&A, where she leads both divestitures and integrations. She is honored to be the co-leader for the women's Business Resource Group. Ms. Skala also serves as the immediate Past-President of the Board of Directors for Snow City Arts, whose mission is to inspire and educate children in hospitals through the arts. She resides in Illinois with her husband and son.

 Marshall Sonenshine is Chairman and Managing Partner of Sonenshine Partners. Sonenshine began his pursuit of the M&A middle market industry at Solomon Brothers where he handled M&A and corporate finance assignments. In 1996, he joined BT Wolfensohn as a partner handling media and transportation M&A. He is known for advising transactions for some of the largest companies in the nation. Sonenshine has led teams closing deals as large as $20 billion. He is also Professor of Finance at Columbia Business School. In addition, Sonenshine is Vice Chairman of the Board of Arts Connection, and trustee and member of the Executive of the International Center of Photography.

Phillip D. Torrence is a Partner at Honigman Miller Schwartz and Cohn LLP, office managing partner in the firm's Kalamazoo, Michigan, office, and leader of the firm's Financial Institutions Practice and Securities and Corporate Governance Practice. He represents public and private companies in a wide range of industries, including the medical device and life-sciences industries and the banking sector. Mr. Torrence counsels public and private companies in initial public offerings and direct public offerings, confidentially marketed public offerings, and debt or hybrid securities secondary offerings of equity. He has handled more than 40 bank merger and acquisition transactions and more than 100 mergers and acquisitions in diverse industry sectors. Mr. Torrence earned a JD from the University of Utah and a B.A. from Hope College.

Robert S. Townsend is Co-Chair of Morrison & Foerster's Global M&A Practice Group. He has represented clients in more than 200 public and private company acquisitions, strategic alliances, and financings, including numerous multibillion-dollar transactions. He often advises on complex cross-border transactions, and he represents companies operating in a range of industries, including technology, telecommunications, media, consumer products, healthcare, life sciences, cleantech, energy, and wine. In addition to his extensive M&A experience, Mr. Townsend has represented numerous public and private companies and investors in corporate and finance matters and regularly advises CEOs, Boards of Directors and Special Committees in strategic and corporate governance issues.

Savio Tung is Chief Investment Officer of Investcorp, a global alternative investment company. Before joining Investcorp as a founder in 1984, Mr. Tung was a senior banker at Chase Manhattan Bank in New York, Bahrain, Abu Dhabi and London. He was a key officer in establishing Chase's Bahrain office and marketing presence in the Persian Gulf. He is an independent non-executive director of the Bank of China/Hong Kong, Ltd.

David P. Wales is Practice Leader, Global Antitrust and Competition, Jones Day in Washington, DC. From 2001 to 2003 he was counsel to the assistant attorney general in the US Department of Justice's Antitrust Division, overseeing all antitrust matters before the agency, including the landmark US v Microsoft case as well as the DIRECTV/Echostar merger and Northrop Grumman's acquisition of TRW. From 2008 until 2009 he oversaw all of the US Federal Trade Commission's antitrust enforcement as acting director of the Bureau of Competition. Prominent cases include Whole Foods' acquisition of Wild Oats and Inova's acquisition of Prince William Hospital. Mr. Wales has testified on antitrust issues before the US Congress and the Antitrust Modernization Committee.

 Raymond Weisner is Senior Vice President and Managing Director at Valuation Research Corporation, responsible for the development and quality execution of client engagements in their New York office. A member of Financial Executives International (FEI), Mr. Weisner has served as chief financial officer of two private companies. Prior to joining Valuation Research, Mr. Weisner also held management and business development positions. In addition, he has provided consulting services to numerous companies, advising on business plans and financial models, and acting as a liaison for the raising of angel and venture capital. Mr. Weisner earned his master of business administration degree in finance and marketing from The University of Connecticut, and undergraduate degrees in architecture and science from Rensselaer Polytechnic Institute.

 Scott Werry is Partner at Altas Partners, a private equity firm in Toronto. Before joining Altas, he worked at Providence Equity Partners in New York, where he focused on opportunities in the communications and business services sectors. Prior to Providence, Mr. Werry worked at McColl Partners, a middle market investment banking firm, where he advised corporations and large family-owned business in M&A and financing transactions.

INDEX

A Bow to the Valued Contributors of Best Practices of the Best Dealmakers, 2nd Edition

Best Practices of the Best Dealmakers, 3rd Edition is the latest installment in a series dedicated to exploring the methodologies of successful M&A practitioners. The objective of the Best Practices of the Best Dealmakers series is to investigate key dealmaking challenges as seen through the eyes of expert practitioners, providing M&A professionals with an essential reference tool.

We are indebted and proud to recognize the following 56 professionals who contributed their valuable insights to Best Practices of the Best Dealmakers, 2nd Edition:

- Alan Annex, Chair of Corporate and Restructuring Practice, Greenberg Traurig
- René-Pierre Azria, Senior Partner, LionTree
- Corinne Ball, Partner and Co-Head of the Global Business Restructuring and Reorganization Practice, Jones Day
- Gregory Bedrosian, Co-Founder, CEO and Managing Partner, Redwood Capital Group
- Lorie Beers, Senior Managing Director, Variant Capital Advisors
- Leigh Brand, Founder and Chairman, Brand Consulting Group Inc.
- Randy Bullard, Department Chair, Greenberg Traurig
- David Carpenter, Partner, Mayer Brown
- Kathryn Coleman, Partner, Hughes, Hubbard & Reed
- Brian Demkowicz, Managing Partner and Co-Founder, Huron Capital Partners
- Christian Deseglise, Managing Director, HSBC Global Asset Management
- Alex Dunev, Senior President, Tegris Advisors
- Brent Earles, Senior Vice President, Allegiance Capital Corporation
- Scott W. Edwards, Managing Director and Head of Investor Relations and Communications, Sun Capital Partners
- Amy Edgy Ferber, Partner, Jones Day
- Michael Fieldstone, Partner, Aterian Investment Partners
- Scott George, Senior Vice President, Hillenbrand
- Dennis Graham, Consulting Partner, Plante Morans
- Alex Hao, Partner, Jun He
- Gilbert Harrison, Founder and Chairman, Financo Inc.

- Thomas Hayes III, Founding Principal, NHB Advisors
- Tom Herd, Managing Partner, Accenture
- David Hull, Partner, Renovo Capital
- Philip J. Isom, Managing Director, KPMG Corporate Finance LLC
- Roberto Kampfner, Partner, White and Case
- Albert A. Kass, Vice President, Kurtzman Carson Consultants
- Peter S. Kaufman, President, Gordian Group
- Thomas J. Kenny, Senior Vice President, Murray Devine
- Rodger R. Krouse, Co-CEO, Sun Capital Partners
- Marlen Kruzhkov, Partner, Gusrae, Kaplan Nusbaum PLLC
- Larry Lattig, President, Mesirow Financial Consulting
- Sharon Levine, Partner, Lowenstein Sandler
- Dr.Cindy Ma, Managing Director, Houlihan Lokey
- Justine Mannering, Director, BDA Partners
- Timothy Meyer, Managing Director, Gores Group
- Howard Morgan, Co-President, Castle Harlan
- Chuck Moritt, Senior Partner, Mercer Consulting
- Martin Okner, Co-Founder and Managing Director, SHM & Co.
- Nancy Peterman, Chair of Business Reorganization and Financial Restructuring Practice, Greenberg Traurig
- Gerard Picco, Senior Director, Avison & Young
- Christopher Picone, Founder, President and General Counsel, Picone Advisory Group
- Bob Profusek, Partner and Chair of the Global M&A Practice, Jones Day
- Eric Reiter, Partner, Brentwood Associates
- William Repko, Senior Advisor and Co-Founder, Evercore Partners
- Andrew Rice, Senior Vice President, Jordan Company
- Jonathan Rouner, Head of International M&A, Nomura
- Durc Savini, Managing Director and Head of the Restructuring and Recapitalization Group, PJSC
- Dennis Shaugnessy, Advisor, FTI Consulting, Inc.
- Steve Shimshak, Partner, Paul Weiss
- Mark Sirower, Principal, Deloitte Consulting LLP
- David Smalstig, Senior Managing Director, FTI Consulting
- Duncan Smithson, Partner, Mercer
- Marshall Sonenshine, Chairman, Sonenshine Partners
- Marc Suidan, Partner, PwC
- Malcolm Tuesley, Counsel, Skadden, Arps, Slate, Meagher & Flom LLP
- Mark Zeffiro, CFO, TriMas

MERRILL DATASITE®

About Merrill DataSite®

Merrill DataSite is a secure virtual data room (VDR) solution that optimizes the due diligence process by providing a highly efficient and secure method for sharing key business information between multiple parties. Merrill DataSite provides unlimited access for users worldwide, as well as real-time activity reports, site-wide search at the document level, enhanced communications through the Q&A feature and superior project management service – all of which help reduce transaction time and expense. Merrill DataSite's multilingual support staff is available from anywhere in the world, 24/7, and can have your VDR up and running with thousands of pages loaded within 24 hours or less.

With its deep roots in transaction and compliance services, Merrill has a cultural,organization-wide discipline in the management and processing of confidential content. Merrill DataSite is the first VDR provider to understand customer and industry needs by earning an ISO/IEC 27001 certificate of registration – the highest standard for information security – and is currently the world's only VDR certified for operations in the United States, Europe and Asia. Merrill DataSite's ISO certification is available for review at www.datasite.com/security.htm.

As the leading provider of VDR solutions, Merrill DataSite has empowered more than two million unique visitors to perform electronic due diligence on thousands of transactions totaling trillions of dollars in asset value. Merrill DataSite VDR solution has become an essential tool in an efficient and legally defensible process forcompleting multiple types of financial transactions.

Learn more by visiting www.datasite.com today.

About Merrill Corporation

Merrill Corporation (www.merrillcorp.com) provides technology-enabled platforms for content sharing, regulated communications and compliance services. Merrill clients trust our innovative cloud-based applications and deep subject expertise to successfully navigate the secure sharing of their most sensitive content, perfect and distribute critical financial and regulatory disclosures, and create customized communications across stakeholders. With more than 3,800 people in 47 locations worldwide, Merrill clients turn to us when their need to manage complex content intersects with the need to collaborate securely around the globe.

THE **M&A** ADVISOR

The M&A Advisor was founded in 1998 to offer insights and intelligence on mergers and acquisitions through the industry's leading publication. Over the past seventeen years, we have established the world's premier leadership organization of M&A, Turnaround and Financing professionals. Today, we have the privilege of presenting, publishing, recognizing the achievements of, and facilitating connections among the industry's top performers throughout the world with a comprehensive range of services including:

M&A Advisor Forums and Summits. Exclusive gatherings of global "thought leaders."
M&A Market Intel. Comprehensive research, analysis, and reporting on the industry.
M&A.TV. Reporting on the key industry events and interviewing the newsmakers.
M&A Advisor Awards. Recognizing excellence of the leading firms and professionals.
M&A Connects. Direct connection service for dealmakers, influencers and service providers.
M&A Links. The largest global network of M&A, Financing and Turnaround professionals.

For additional information about The M&A Advisor's leadership services, contact lpisareva@maadvisor.com.